ideals®

Pies and Pastries
COOKBOOK

by Naomi Arbit and June Turner

Ideals Publishing Corp.
Milwaukee, Wisconsin

Contents

Cover recipes: Cherry-Raspberry Pie, page 29
Napoleons, page 43

ISBN 0-8249-3011-8
Copyright © MCMLXXXII by Naomi Arbit and June Turner
All rights reserved.
Printed and bound in the United States of America.

Published by Ideals Publishing Corporation
11315 Watertown Plank Road
Milwaukee, Wisconsin 53226
Published simultaneously in Canada

Pie & Pastry Basics

We have gathered the best and most interesting recipes for pies, pastries and small sweets. This distinctive collection includes old favorites, updated and simplified whenever possible, and new recipes which will tempt you because they sound so good.

The directions are simple, the ingredients are readily available and the results will be sensational. The recipes range from a simple custard for a pie filling to an elaborate towering confection called Croquembouche, a show-off centerpiece for the table at a reception or high tea. You will also find fudgy brownies, chewy bars, tiny one-bite tarts, luscious cream puffs and flaky pastries.

The following introduction features basic steps along with diagrams to ensure success in preparing delicious pies and pastries.

Mixing Pastry for Pies and Tarts

1. Sift flour before measuring it. Spoon it into a measuring cup; *do not pack it.* Use a knife to level off the flour. Combine the flour with salt in a sifter. Sift into a large mixing bowl.

2A. Cut ½ of shortening into flour mixture with a pastry blender until the mixture looks like cornmeal. Cut in the remaining shortening until the mixture resembles peas.

2B. When using liquid shortening, mix it into the dry ingredients with a fork until the mixture looks like cornmeal.

3. Add liquid, 1 tablespoon at a time, sprinkling it over the flour-shortening mixture. As the water is added, toss the mixture with a fork until all flour particles are moistened and the mixture begins to leave the sides of the bowl. Add just enough liquid to hold the ingredients together.

4A. Gather the dough together with your fingers and press into a ball, handling the dough no more than necessary. Wrap it in plastic wrap and chill at least 1 hour *or* as the recipe directs.

4B. Remove the dough from the refrigerator 1 hour before rolling.

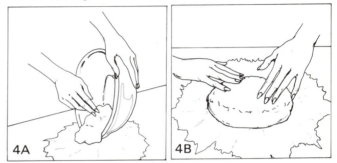

Rolling and Fitting Pastry for Pies and Tarts

1. Lightly flour a wooden board *or* pastry cloth and the rolling pin. When rolling double-crust pies, divide the dough into two balls, making one slightly smaller than the other.

2. Flatten the ball of dough slightly. Roll lightly from the center of the dough out, slightly lifting the rolling pin as it nears the edge of the dough. Be careful not to use too much pressure during rolling or the dough will be stretched. Periodically it may be necessary to lift the edges of the dough to sparingly sprinkle more flour under the dough to prevent it from sticking to the board. Periodic reflouring of the rolling pin also may be necessary. If the edges of the dough begin to crack or tear during rolling, pinch them together. It is better to have a few mended tears than to reroll a crust.

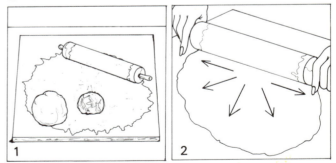

3. Keep the dough circular during rolling. Roll the dough ⅛-inch thick and about 2 inches larger than the inverted pie pan.

4. Gently loosen the dough from the board *or* cloth. Fold the dough in half. Lay the fold of the dough in the center of the pie pan.

Pie & Pastry Basics

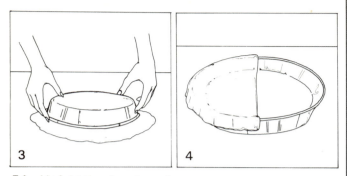

3

4

5A. Unfold the dough and ease it into the bottom and up the side of the pan. *Do not* stretch the dough.

5B. For a single-crust pie, trim the dough to a 1-inch overhang. Fold the dough overhang under to make a high rim. Flute as desired (see page 5). Fill the crust and bake according to recipe directions. For a baked crust, follow the directions in step 1 of Baking Pie and Tart Crusts (see page 5).

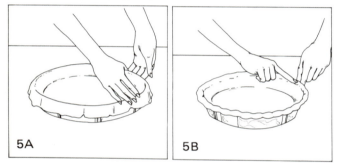

5A

5B

5C. For a double-crust pie, fit the bottom crust in the pie pan as directed in steps 3 and 4, trimming the dough overhang to ½-inch. Fill the crust as directed in the recipe. Roll the top crust according to directions in steps 2 and 3, making it large enough to extend ½-inch beyond the edge of the pie pan. Fold the dough in half, then in half again. Make several slits near the center of the fold so steam can escape during baking. Moisten the edge of the bottom overhang with water.

5D. Carefully place the folded top dough on ¼ of the pie. Unfold so that it completely covers the pie. Fold the top overhang under the bottom overhang. Press together with fingertips to build high rim. Flute as desired (see page 5). Bake according to recipe directions. To prevent edge of crust from becoming too brown, cover it with 1½-inch strip of foil, remove the foil during the last 15 minutes of baking to brown the crust edge.

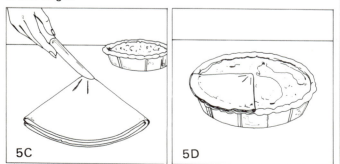

5C

5D

6A. For a lattice top on a pie, roll the top crust and cut into ½-inch strips using a sharp knife. For a pretty edge, use a pastry wheel. Lay half of the strips 1 inch apart over the filled pie. (Dough strips can be twisted if desired.) Starting at the center of the pie, place 1 strip of dough over the filling in the opposite direction of the other dough strips.

6B. Weave the strip through the other strips on the pie. Continue adding and weaving the strips until the lattice is complete. Lift all of the strip ends to moisten the bottom overhang with water. Lay the strip ends on the bottom overhang and trim the ends of the strips even with the edge of the pie pan, pressing the strips into the bottom crust.

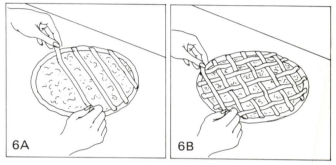

6A

6B

6C. Fold the bottom overhang over the strips to form rim. Flute as desired (see page 5).

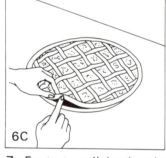

6C

7. For tarts, roll the dough according to step 2. Cut the dough 1 inch larger than the diameter of the inverted tart tin, muffin tin or custard cup. Ease the dough into the tin, pressing it to fit on the bottom and up the side of the tin. *Do not* stretch the dough. Trim the dough to ½-inch overhang. Fold under to build high rim. Fill and bake according to recipe directions. For baked tart crusts, follow directions in step 2 of Baking Pie and Tart Crusts (see page 5).

8. For pastry made with oil instead of shortening, roll the dough between two long strips of waxed paper. Wipe the table with a damp cloth to keep the paper from slipping during rolling. Peel off the top paper and place the dough in the pan, paper-side-up. Peel off the paper and fit the dough loosely into the pan. Trim the dough leaving ½-inch overhang. Fold under to form high rim. Flute as desired (see page 5). Fill and bake according to recipe directions. For baked crust, follow the directions in step 1 of Baking Pie and Tart Crusts (see page 5). If using a double-crust recipe, roll the top crust in the same manner, place it on the filled pie, cut steam vents, flute edge and bake the pie according to recipe directions.

9. Crumb crusts are mixed and patted into the pie pan. An easy way to form a crumb crust is to place the crumb mixture in the pan, distributing the crumbs evenly. Press another pie pan of the same size firmly into the crumbs to distribute them evenly. Brush away any excess crumbs that are forced to the top edge. Crumb crusts need not be baked before filling, but should be chilled thoroughly before the filling is added so the filling will not soak into the crust. Crumb crusts should be baked in a preheated 300° oven 15 minutes. Cool before filling.

Meringue Crusts and Toppings

1A. To shape and bake a meringue piecrust, cover a baking sheet with brown wrapping paper. Draw a 9-inch circle on the paper using a plate as a guide.

1B. Shape the meringue on the circle. Make the center of the crust about 1 inch thick. The rim should be about 2 inches high. Bake 1 hour in preheated 250° oven.

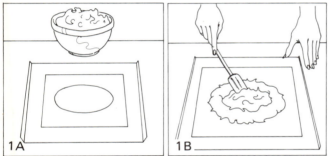

1C. Turn off the heat, open the oven door and leave the crust in the oven until it cools, about 1 hour. Remove from the paper, place on serving plate and fill as desired.

2. To make a meringue topping for a pie, spread the meringue evenly over the pie filling, starting at the edge of the pie to seal the meringue to the crust. Don't leave uncovered spaces between the crust and the meringue or the meringue will shrink away from the crust during baking. Swirl the rest of the meringue on the pie evenly in an attractive manner. Bake in a preheated 350° oven 12 to 15 minutes *or* until the meringue is baked to the desired brown color. Cool at room temperature away from draft.

3. Making meringue is easy if a few simple steps are followed:
A. Always have the egg whites at room temperature.
B. Beat the egg whites until they are foamy before adding the cream of tartar or salt.
C. Add the sugar gradually and only after the egg whites have been beaten to soft peaks.
D. Have all utensils absolutely free of grease.
E. Be sure there is no egg yolk in the whites or the whites will not beat to their fullest volume.
F. Excess sugar, beaten into meringue, will cause the meringue to be gummy and to "bead" after baking.

Fluting Piecrusts

Pies have fluted edges for decoration and to provide a high rim to help contain the contents of the pie during baking. There are several ways to flute a pie:

1. Fold the dough overhang under to build a high rim. Supporting the outer edge of the high rim with your fingers, press the tines of a fork against the dough all around the inside of the rim. To prevent the fork from sticking to the dough, occasionally dip it in flour. For variety, only press the fork at intervals around the edge of the dough, leaving some parts plain.

2. For a shell effect, fold the dough overhang under to build a high rim. Place the right thumb on the edge of the pie rim. Press and twist the knuckle of the right index finger toward the thumb, forming a ripple effect. Repeat all around pie.

3. For a ruffle effect, fold the dough overhang under to build a high rim. Place a floured left index finger inside the rim. With the right thumb and index finger on the outside of the rim, press and pinch the dough into a V shape, spacing about ½ inch apart. Pinch flutes to make definite points, if desired.

Baking Pie and Tart Crusts

1. For a single crust, flute the edges as described (see page 5). Prick the bottom and sides of the dough with the tines of a fork. Chill the dough 30 minutes. Line the dough with foil *or* parchment paper. (*Do not* use waxed paper.) Fill the crust with dry beans *or* rice to weight down the crust and prevent it from ballooning *or* pulling away from the pan during baking. Bake in preheated 450° oven 12 to 15 minutes. Remove the beans *or* rice and foil *or* parchment paper. (These can be reused.) Bake 4 to 5 minutes longer until the crust is dry and light brown. Cool before filling.

2. For tarts, prick the bottom and sides of the dough with the tines of a fork. Chill 30 minutes. Bake in preheated 450° oven 10 to 12 minutes. Cool on rack. Remove crusts from tins *or* cups. Cool completely before filling. *Note:* Only prick the bottom and sides of pie and tart crusts that are to be baked and then filled. Never prick the dough that will be baked along with a pie filling.

Piecrusts

Basic Piecrust

Makes 1 9- or 10-inch single crust *or* 1 9- or 10-inch double crust.
Preparation Time: 30 minutes plus 1 hour to chill.

  1¼ cups flour
  ½ teaspoon salt
  ½ cup vegetable shortening
  3 to 4 tablespoons cold water

Sift flour and salt in bowl. Cut in ½ shortening with pastry blender until mixture resembles cornmeal. Cut in remaining ½ shortening until mixture resembles peas. Add water 1 tablespoon at a time, mixing lightly with fork until dough comes together and leaves side of bowl. Form into ball, wrap in plastic wrap and chill 1 hour. Follow steps 1 through 5A of Rolling and Fitting Pastry for Pies and Tarts, using 9-inch pie pan.

Note: For baked crust, follow directions in step 1 of Baking Pie and Tart Crusts. Cool before filling.

Variations

10-inch Single Piecrust: Prepare as above using 1½ cups flour, ¾ teaspoon salt, ½ cup plus 1 tablespoon vegetable shortening and 3 tablespoons cold water.

9-inch Double Piecrust: Prepare as above using 2 cups flour, 1 teaspoon salt, ⅔ cup plus 2 tablespoons vegetable shortening and ¼ cup cold water.

10-inch Double Piecrust: Prepare as above using 3 cups flour, 1½ teaspoons salt, 1 cup plus 2 tablespoons vegetable shortening and 6 tablespoons cold water.

No-Roll Piecrust

Makes 1 9-inch single crust.
Preparation Time: 30 minutes plus 1 hour to chill.

  6 tablespoons butter *or* margarine
  1 cup flour
  2 to 3 tablespoons cold water

Cut butter into flour in bowl with pastry blender until mixture resembles coarse crumbs. Sprinkle with water; blend until mixture forms ball. Press into bottom and up side of 9-inch pie pan, using lightly floured hands. Chill before baking.

Note: For baked crust, follow directions in step 1 of Baking Pie and Tart Crusts. Cool before filling.

Vegetable Oil Piecrust

Makes 1 9-inch single crust *or* 1 10-inch single crust *or* 1 9-inch double crust.
Preparation Time: 30 minutes plus 1 hour to chill.

  1⅓ cups flour
  ½ teaspoon salt
  ⅓ cup vegetable oil
  3 tablespoons cold milk

Sift flour and salt in bowl. Mix in oil and milk with fork until mixture resembles cornmeal. Form into ball and wrap in plastic wrap. Chill 30 minutes. Follow directions in step 5E of Rolling and Fitting Pastry for Pies and Tarts, using 9-inch pie pan. For baked crust, follow directions in step 1 of Baking Pie and Tart Crusts. Cool before filling.

Note: For 10-inch single crust *or* 9-inch double crust, prepare as above using 2 cups flour, ½ teaspoon salt, ½ cup vegetable oil and ¼ cup cold milk.

Butter Piecrust

Makes 1 9-inch single crust.
Preparation Time: 30 minutes plus 1 hour to chill.

  1 cup flour
  3 tablespoons granulated sugar
  ⅓ cup butter
  1 egg yolk, lightly beaten

Sift flour and sugar in bowl. Cut in ½ butter with pastry blender until mixture resembles cornmeal. Cut in remaining ½ of butter until mixture resembles peas. Stir in yolk. Form into ball; press into bottom and up side of 9-inch pie pan.

Note: For baked crust, follow directions in step 1 of Baking Pie and Tart Crusts, using preheated 400° oven. Cool before filling.

From top: Basic Piecrust, this page;
Meringue Crust, see Almond Meringue Piecrust,
but omit almonds, page 31;
Lattice Piecrust, see Basic Double Piecrust,
this page; then see introduction
for lattice top instructions.

Piecrusts

Graham Cracker Crust

Makes 1 9-inch crust *or* 1 10-inch crust.
Preparation Time: 20 minutes.

1½ cups fine graham cracker crumbs
2 tablespoons granulated sugar
6 tablespoons butter *or* margarine, melted

Preheat oven to 375°. Mix all ingredients together in bowl. Press firmly on bottom and up side of 9-inch pie pan. Bake 6 to 8 minutes. Cool before filling.

Note: For 10-inch crust, prepare as above using 2 cups fine graham cracker crumbs, ¼ cup granulated sugar and ½ cup melted butter *or* margarine.

Boiling Water Piecrust

Makes 1 9-inch double crust.
Preparation Time: 30 minutes plus 1 hour to chill.

⅔ cup vegetable shortening
⅓ cup boiling water
2 cups flour
½ teaspoon salt

Beat shortening in large bowl. Add boiling water; mix with fork until smooth and creamy. Mix sifted flour and salt together; add to shortening, mixing with fork. Wrap ball of dough in plastic wrap; chill 30 minutes. Follow step 5E of Rolling and Fitting Pastry for Pies and Tarts, using 9-inch pie pan.

Note: For baked crust, follow step 1 of Baking Pie and Tart Crusts. Cool before filling.

Cheese Piecrust

This tangy cheese crust complements apple or pear pies.

Makes 1 9-inch *or* 1 10-inch crust with lattice top.
Preparation Time: 30 minutes plus 1 hour to chill.

1⅔ cups flour
½ teaspoon salt
⅛ teaspoon cayenne pepper
1 cup grated sharp Cheddar cheese
½ cup butter *or* margarine
5 to 6 tablespoons water

Sift flour, salt and pepper in bowl; mix in cheese. Cut in ½ butter with pastry blender until mixture resembles cornmeal. Cut in remaining butter until mixture resembles peas. Add water, 1 table-spoon at a time, until dough holds together. Chill 30 minutes. Follow steps 1 through 4, 5A and 5C of Rolling and Fitting Pastry for Pies and Tarts, using 9-inch pie pan. Bake according to filling recipe directions.

Note: For 10-inch crust with lattice top, prepare as above using 2 cups flour, ½ teaspoon salt, ⅛ teaspoon cayenne pepper, 1½ cups grated sharp Cheddar cheese, ½ cup plus 2 tablespoons butter *or* margarine and 6 to 7 tablespoons ice water.

Buttery Piecrust

Makes 1 9-inch single crust *or* 1 10-inch single crust.
Preparation Time: 30 minutes plus 1 hour to chill.

1 cup flour
2 tablespoons granulated sugar
½ cup butter

Sift flour and sugar in bowl. Cut in butter with pastry blender until mixture resembles cornmeal. Mix just until dough forms. Press evenly over bottom and up side of 9- or 10-inch pie pan. (Dough will be easier to press into pan with floured fingertips.)

Note: For baked crust, follow directions in step 1 of Baking Pie and Tart Crusts. Cool before filling.

Foolproof Piecrust

Makes 1 9-inch single crust.
Preparation Time: 30 minutes plus 1 hour to chill.

1 cup flour
¼ teaspoon salt
½ cup butter *or* margarine, softened

Sift flour and salt in bowl. Cut in softened butter using pastry blender. Mix until dough forms ball. Pat dough into 9-inch pie pan. Chill 1 hour before filling.

Note: For baked crust, follow directions in step 1 of Baking Pie and Tart Crusts, using preheated 400° oven. Cool before filling.

Toasted Almond Crust

Makes 1 9-inch crust.
Preparation Time: 15 minutes plus 2 hours to chill.

- ½ cup butter *or* margarine
- ½ cup chopped almonds
- ½ cup granulated sugar
- 1 cup flour
- ¼ teaspoon ground cinnamon

Melt butter in large skillet; stir in almonds and sauté until golden. Remove from heat; stir in sugar, flour and cinnamon until mixture is golden and crumbly. Press into 9-inch pie plate. Chill 2 hours before filling.

Cereal Piecrust

Any puffed or flaked cold cereal can be used to make this tasty piecrust.

Makes 1 9-inch crust *or* 1 10-inch crust.
Preparation Time: 25 minutes.

- 6 cups cereal flakes *or* puffs, to make
  1½ cups crumbs
- 6 tablespoons butter *or* margarine, melted
- 2 tablespoons granulated sugar
- ½ teaspoon ground cinnamon

Preheat oven to 325°. Mix all ingredients in bowl. Press firmly onto bottom and up side of 9-inch pie pan. Press down firmly on crust with another pie pan. Bake 10 to 12 minutes. Cool before filling.

Note: For 10-inch crust, prepare as above, using 8 cups cereal to make 2 cups crumbs, ¼ cup granulated sugar, ½ cup butter *or* margarine, melted and ½ teaspoon ground cinnamon.

Chocolate Crumb Crust

Makes 1 9-inch crust *or* 1 10-inch crust.
Preparation Time: 20 minutes.

- 1½ cups chocolate wafer crumbs
- ½ teaspoon ground cinnamon
- 6 tablespoons butter *or* margarine, melted
- ¼ cup chopped nuts, optional

Preheat oven to 375°. Mix all ingredients together in bowl. Press firmly on bottom and up side of 9-inch pie pan. Bake 6 to 8 minutes. Cool before filling.

Note: For 10-inch crust, prepare as above, using 2 cups chocolate wafer crumbs, ½ teaspoon ground cinnamon, ½ cup butter *or* margarine, melted and ½ cup chopped nuts, optional.

Chocolate-Coconut Crust

Makes 1 9-inch crust *or* 1 10-inch crust.
Preparation Time: 15 minutes.

- 4 ounces sweet chocolate
- 2 tablespoons butter *or* margarine
- 2 cups flaked coconut

Melt chocolate and butter in saucepan over low heat; remove from heat. Stir in coconut. Spread on bottom and up side of 9-inch pie plate. Cool before filling.

Note: For 10-inch crust, prepare as above, using 4 ounces sweet chocolate, ¼ cup butter *or* margarine and 2½ cups flaked coconut.

Coconut Crust

This crust adds a nice crunchy texture to a smooth custard or cream filling.

Makes 1 9-inch crust *or* 1 10-inch crust.
Preparation Time: 25 minutes.

- 2 cups flaked coconut
- ¼ cup butter, softened
- 1 tablespoon flour

Preheat oven to 325°. Mix all ingredients in bowl. Press firmly onto bottom and up side of 9-inch pie pan. Bake 10 to 12 minutes until lightly browned. Cool before filling.

Note: For 10-inch crust, prepare as above, using 2½ cups flaked coconut, 6 tablespoons softened butter and 1½ tablespoons flour.

Cookie Crumb Crust

Makes 1 9-inch crust *or* 1 10-inch crust.
Preparation Time: 25 minutes.

- 1½ cups shortbread, vanilla *or*
  gingersnap cookie crumbs
- 3 tablespoons granulated sugar
- 6 tablespoons butter *or* margarine, melted

Preheat oven to 325°. Mix all ingredients together in bowl. Press onto bottom and up side of 9-inch pie pan. Press down firmly with another pie pan. Bake 10 to 12 minutes. Cool before filling.

Note: For 10-inch crust, prepare as above, using 2 cups cookie crumbs, ¼ cup granulated sugar and ½ cup melted butter *or* margarine.

Angel Pie

Makes 1 9-inch pie.
Preparation Time: 1½ hours plus time to chill.

    3 egg whites, room temperature
    ¼ teaspoon cream of tartar
    ⅛ teaspoon salt
    ½ teaspoon vanilla
    ¾ cup granulated sugar
    ½ cup finely chopped nuts, optional
       Chocolate Filling

Preheat oven to 300°. Beat egg whites in bowl until foamy. Add cream of tartar, salt and vanilla; beat until soft peaks form. Add sugar, 2 tablespoons at a time, beating until stiff peaks form. Fold in nuts. Spread evenly over bottom and up side of 9-inch pie pan. Bake 45 minutes or until just golden. Cool on rack. Fill with Chocolate Filling; chill.

Chocolate Filling

    1 12-ounce package semisweet chocolate chips or
    2 4-ounce bars sweet baking chocolate
    3 tablespoons boiling water
    1 teaspoon instant coffee granules
    ¼ cup boiling water
    1 cup whipping cream, whipped
    1 teaspoon vanilla

Melt chocolate with 3 tablespoons boiling water in saucepan. Stir in coffee granules and ¼ cup boiling water. Cool. Fold in whipped cream and vanilla; stir until smooth.

Apricot Pie

Preparation Time: 1½ hours plus 2 hours to chill.

    1 9-inch baked pastry shell
    ½ cup dried apricots, chopped
    ½ cup water
    1 cup granulated sugar
    ¼ cup cornstarch
    2½ cups milk
    2 egg yolks, lightly beaten
    1 tablespoon butter or margarine
    1 teaspoon orange juice concentrate
    1 cup whipping cream
    2 tablespoons granulated sugar
    ½ teaspoon almond extract
       Ground nutmeg, to garnish

Bring apricots and water to boil in saucepan; cook 20 minutes. Puree in blender or in food processor; set aside. Combine 1 cup sugar and cornstarch in saucepan; gradually add milk. Add egg yolks; cook over medium heat, stirring constantly, until mixture boils 1 minute and thickens. Remove from heat; stir in apricot puree, butter and orange concentrate. Cool slightly; pour into pie shell. Chill 2 hours. Whip cream with 2 tablespoons sugar and almond extract until stiff. Spread over pie. Chill. Sprinkle with nutmeg before serving, if desired.

Cannoli Cream Pie

Preparation Time: 1 hour plus chilling time.

    1 9-inch baked pastry shell or crumb crust
    1 3¾-ounce package instant vanilla pudding mix,
       prepared with 1½ cups milk
    1 16-ounce container small curd cottage cheese
    ½ cup confectioners' sugar
    1 teaspoon vanilla
    ½ teaspoon almond extract
    ¼ cup semisweet chocolate chips
    ½ cup finely chopped almonds or pistachios
    ½ cup whipping cream, whipped
    5 to 6 maraschino cherries, drained and halved

Prepare pudding mix according to package directions; chill 30 minutes. Puree cottage cheese, confectioners' sugar and flavorings in blender or food processor. Fold cheese mixture, chocolate chips and nuts into pudding. Pour into pie shell. Frost with whipped cream. Decorate with cherries. Chill.

Chocolate Marble Pie

Luscious and beautiful, this easy-to-make pie starts with pudding mix.

Preparation Time: 50 minutes.

    1 9-inch baked pie crust
    1 3¾-ounce instant chocolate pudding mix
    1 teaspoon instant coffee granules
    1 tablespoon butter
    1 teaspoon vanilla
    ½ cup whipping cream, whipped

Prepare pudding mix according to package directions. Add coffee granules, butter and vanilla; cool. Pour into pie shell. Spread whipped cream over top; swirl into filling with a rubber spatula to create a marbled effect. Chill.

Cream Pies

Chocolate Whipped Cream Pie

There are no eggs in this delicious pie.

Preparation Time: 1 hour plus time to chill.

- 1 9-inch baked Vegetable Oil Piecrust (Recipe on page 6)
- ⅔ cup granulated sugar
- ¼ cup unsweetened cocoa
- ⅛ teaspoon salt
- 1 cup milk
- 1 tablespoon unflavored gelatin softened in ¼ cup cold water
- ½ teaspoon instant coffee granules
- 1 cup whipping cream, whipped
  Whipped cream *or* chocolate curls, optional

Combine sugar, cocoa and salt in saucepan. Stir in milk; heat to boiling, stirring constantly; remove from heat. Stir in softened gelatin and coffee granules. Chill until mixture begins to thicken. Fold in whipped cream; pour into crust. Chill until firm. Garnish with additional whipped cream or chocolate curls, if desired.

Lemon Cream Pie

Quick to prepare, this Lemon Cream Pie requires no cooking.

Preparation Time: 20 minutes plus 3 hours to chill.

- 1 9-inch baked crumb crust
- 1 14-ounce can sweetened condensed milk
- ½ cup lemon juice
- 1 tablespoon grated lemon rind
- 3 egg whites, room temperature
- 2 tablespoons granulated sugar

Combine milk, lemon juice and rind in bowl. Beat egg whites in separate bowl until foamy. Gradually add sugar; beat until stiff peaks form. Gently fold egg whites into lemon mixture; pour into crust. Chill 3 hours or until set.

Sherry Vanilla Cream Pie

Preparation Time: 1 hour plus chilling time.

- 1 9-inch baked Graham Cracker Crust (Recipe on page 8) *or* Chocolate Crumb Crust (Recipe on page 9)
- 1 3¾-ounce package instant French vanilla pudding mix
- 1½ cups milk
- ¼ cup sherry
- 1 cup whipping cream, whipped

Prepare pudding mix with 1½ cups milk according to package directions. Stir in sherry; chill 30 minutes. Gently fold in whipped cream; pour into crust. Chill.

Note: Pie can be topped with fresh fruit, shaved semisweet chocolate *or* any fruit glaze.

Chocolate Silk Pie

This pie is smooth as silk.

Preparation Time: 40 minutes plus 3 hours to chill.

- 1 9-inch baked pastry shell
- 1 cup butter, softened
- 1½ cups granulated sugar
- 4 ounces unsweetened chocolate, melted and cooled
- 1 teaspoon vanilla
- 4 eggs
  Whipped cream, optional

Cream butter and sugar in large bowl. Add chocolate and vanilla; beat at low speed until well blended. Add eggs, 1 at a time, beating 5 minutes after each addition. Pour into pie shell. Chill 3 hours. Top with whipped cream, if desired.

Note: Pie may be frozen if wrapped tightly. Place in refrigerator 2 hours before serving.

Apricot Cream Pie

Preparation Time: 2 hours plus 2 to 3 hours to chill.

- 1 9-inch baked Almond Meringue Pie Shell (Recipe on page 31)
- ½ cup granulated sugar
- ¼ cup cornstarch
  Dash salt
- 3 eggs, lightly beaten
- 1½ cups milk
- ½ teaspoon vanilla
- ½ teaspoon almond extract
- 3 tablespoons butter *or* margarine
- 1 1-pound can apricot halves, drained
- ¼ cup crab apple *or* currant jelly, melted

Combine sugar, cornstarch and salt in saucepan; add eggs and milk. Cook over medium heat, whisking constantly, until mixture comes to a boil. Boil, whisking constantly, 1 minute. Remove from heat; whisk gently until mixture cools slightly. Stir in flavorings and butter. Cool 1 hour. Pour into crust. Chill 2 to 3 hours. At serving time, arrange apricot halves, upside down, on top of pie filling. Drizzle melted jelly over fruit.

Chocolate Custard Cream Pie

Preparation Time: 45 minutes plus chilling time.

  1 9-inch baked pastry shell *or* crumb crust
1½ cups granulated sugar
  ⅓ cup cornstarch
  ¼ teaspoon salt
  ¼ teaspoon cinnamon, optional
  2 cups milk
  3 eggs, lightly beaten
  2 ounces unsweetened chocolate, melted
  1 teaspoon vanilla
  1 tablespoon butter *or* margarine
    Garnishes, optional

Mix sugar, cornstarch, salt and cinnamon, if desired, in saucepan. Add milk to beaten eggs and slowly stir into dry ingredients. Cook, whisking constantly, over medium heat until mixture comes to a boil; boil 1 minute. Remove from heat; add melted chocolate, vanilla and butter. Gently whisk until mixture cools slightly. Pour into pie shell. Cover filling with plastic wrap. Chill until serving time. Garnish, if desired.

Garnishes

  Whipped cream
  Chocolate curls
  Chopped pecans
  Crushed hard peppermint candies
  Sliced bananas

Strawberry Cream Pie

Preparation Time: 1½ hours plus chilling time.

  1 9-inch baked pastry shell
  1 3¾-ounce package instant French vanilla
    pudding mix
1¼ cups milk
  1 cup dairy sour cream
    Glaze
  2 cups fresh strawberries, hulled

Beat pudding mix, milk and sour cream on low speed of electric mixer for 1 minute. Pour into pie shell; chill. Prepare Glaze. Spread ⅓ Glaze over filling. Cover top of pie with strawberries and top with remaining Glaze. Chill until serving time.

Glaze

  ¼ cup granulated sugar
  2 tablespoons cornstarch
  ⅓ cup water
  ⅓ cup grenadine syrup *or* maraschino cherry juice
  1 tablespoon lemon juice

Mix sugar and cornstarch in saucepan; blend in water, syrup and lemon juice. Cook over medium heat until clear and thickened. Cool, covered, at room temperature.

Custard Cream Pie

Cream fillings are cooked on top of the stove, cooled slightly and poured into a baked, cooled pie shell or crumb crust. They are thickened with a combination of cornstarch and eggs.

Preparation Time: 45 minutes plus chilling time.

  1 9-inch baked pastry shell *or* crumb crust
  ⅔ cup granulated sugar
  ¼ cup cornstarch
  ½ teaspoon salt
  2 cups milk
  3 eggs, lightly beaten
  2 teaspoons vanilla
  2 tablespoons butter *or* margarine
    Garnish, optional

Mix sugar, cornstarch and salt in saucepan. Add milk to beaten eggs and slowly stir into dry ingredients. Cook, whisking constantly, over medium heat until mixture comes to a boil; boil 1 minute. Remove from heat; add vanilla and butter. Gently whisk until mixture cools slightly. Pour into pie shell. Cover filling with plastic wrap. Chill until serving time. Garnish, if desired.

Garnishes

  Whipped cream
  Toasted coconut
  Toasted sliced almonds
  Sliced bananas
  Grated sweet chocolate
  Apricot halves, drained and glazed with ¼ cup
    melted currant jelly

Note: If cream filling becomes lumpy during cooking, press it through a strainer or whirl it in a blender a few seconds, until smooth.

Variation

Butterscotch Custard Cream: Follow instructions for Custard Cream Pie, using 1 cup light brown sugar in place of granulated sugar and reduce vanilla to 1 teaspoon.

* * *

To make chocolate curls, hold a wrapped bar of semisweet chocolate in your hands 2 to 3 minutes to warm it slightly. Unwrap and shave the chocolate onto waxed paper with a vegetable peeler, using long strokes.

Custard Pie

There are two methods for making a custard pie to avoid a soggy crust. Either bake the crust and the custard separately and then slip the custard into the crust just before serving, or partially bake the crust, reduce the heat, add the custard and bake. The pie should be cooled on a rack and served at room temperature within 3 hours of baking or refrigerated until serving time.

Preparation Time: 1 hour plus cooling time.

    1 9-inch baked pastry shell
    3 eggs
    ⅓ cup granulated sugar
      Dash salt
    2 cups milk
    1 teaspoon vanilla
    ¼ teaspoon ground nutmeg

Preheat oven to 325°. Beat eggs in bowl; stir in sugar, salt, milk and vanilla. Pour into well-buttered 9-inch pie pan. Sprinkle top with nutmeg. Place in shallow pan; add hot water halfway up side of pan. Bake 40 to 50 minutes or until knife inserted in center comes out clean. Cool on rack. Just before serving, run spatula around edge of custard. Tilt and slip gently into crust.

Alternate Method: Preheat oven to 450°. Bake 9-inch pastry shell 10 minutes. Reduce heat to 325° and pour custard into pie shell. Bake 20 to 30 minutes or until knife inserted in center comes out clean. Cool on rack.

Variations

Coconut: Add ½ cup plain *or* toasted flaked coconut to custard before baking.

Raisin: Add ½ cup seedless raisins to custard before baking.

Almond: Add ½ cup toasted almonds and ½ teaspoon almond extract to custard before baking.

Fruit Glaze: Spread Blueberry Glaze (Recipe on page 41), Strawberry Glaze (Recipe on page 41) *or* Pineapple Glaze (Recipe on page 41) on cooled pie before serving.

Burnt Sugar: Spread 1 cup light brown sugar evenly in 9-inch circle on buttered foil. Broil 4 inches from heat to caramelize sugar. Cool slightly; slip onto cooled pie.

Rum: Beat 1 cup whipping cream with 2 tablespoons granulated sugar and ½ teaspoon rum flavoring *or* vanilla until stiff. Spread on cooled pie. Garnish with ½ cup grated semisweet chocolate, if desired.

Fresh Fruit: Spoon 2 cups sliced fresh strawberries, bananas, peaches *or* fruit of your choice (sweetened, if necessary) on top of cooled pie.

Sour Cream Pumpkin Pie

This rich pie has a slightly tart flavor.

Preparation Time: 1 hour.

    1 9-inch unbaked pastry shell
    1 cup light brown sugar, packed
    1 tablespoon flour
    ½ teaspoon salt
    1 teaspoon ground ginger
    ½ teaspoon ground nutmeg
    ½ teaspoon ground cloves
    ½ teaspoon ground cinnamon
    1 cup canned pumpkin
    2 eggs, well beaten
    1 cup evaporated milk
    ½ cup dairy sour cream
    ½ cup chopped walnuts

Preheat oven to 400°. Mix brown sugar, flour, salt and spices in bowl; add remaining ingredients and mix well. Pour into crust. Bake 40 to 50 minutes or until knife inserted in center comes out clean. Cool on rack.

Walnut Pie

Preparation Time: 1 hour, 15 minutes.

    1 9-inch unbaked pastry shell
    ¼ cup butter *or* margarine
    ½ cup dark corn syrup
    ¼ cup sherry
    1 cup granulated sugar
    3 eggs, lightly beaten
    1 teaspoon vanilla
    1 cup chopped walnuts
    1 cup whipped cream, optional

Preheat oven to 350°. Melt butter in saucepan. Remove from heat and stir in corn syrup, sherry, sugar, eggs and vanilla. Sprinkle nuts on pie shell; pour egg mixture over nuts. Bake 50 to 60 minutes or until knife inserted in custard comes out clean. Cool on rack. Garnish with whipped cream dollops, if desired.

Custard Pies

Date-Nut Pie

Preparation Time: 30 minutes plus 3 hours to chill.

- 1 9-inch baked pastry shell
- 2 cups milk
- ¼ cup butter *or* margarine
- 2 eggs, lightly beaten
- 1 cup light brown sugar, packed
- ⅓ cup cornstarch
- 1 teaspoon vanilla
- 1 cup whipping cream, whipped
- ½ cup chopped dates *or* 1 cup raisins
- ½ cup chopped walnuts

Combine milk, butter, eggs, brown sugar and cornstarch in saucepan. Cook over medium heat, stirring constantly with whisk, until mixture comes to a boil; boil 1 minute. Remove from heat, add vanilla and cool, whisking gently a few minutes. Chill 2 hours. Fold whipped cream, dates and walnuts into custard; spoon into pie shell. Chill 1 hour.

Basic Cheese Pie

Preparation Time: 1 hour, 10 minutes.

- 1 9-inch unbaked pastry shell *or* baked crumb crust, chilled
- 1 8-ounce package cream cheese, softened
- ½ cup granulated sugar
- 2 tablespoons flour
- 3 eggs
- ⅓ cup milk
- 1 teaspoon vanilla
  Topping

Preheat oven to 350°. Beat cream cheese in bowl until smooth; add sugar gradually, beating constantly. Stir in flour and eggs; beat in milk and vanilla until all traces of cheese disappear (filling will be liquid). Pour into pie shell. Bake 40 minutes or until firm, delicate brown and tip of knife inserted in center comes out clean. Spread Topping on top of pie; bake 10 minutes. Chill.

Topping

- 1 cup dairy sour cream
- 2 tablespoons granulated sugar
- ½ teaspoon vanilla

Combine all ingredients.

Note: For variation omit Topping; spread cool pie with a fruit glaze (see page 41). Chill.

Chocolate Mousse-Cheese Pie

Preparation Time: 1 hour, 15 minutes plus 3 to 4 hours to chill.

- 1 10-inch unbaked pastry shell *or* crumb crust of your choice
- 2 8-ounce packages cream cheese, softened
- ½ cup granulated sugar
- 2 eggs
- 1 cup semisweet chocolate chips, melted
- 2 tablespoons cream *or* milk
- 1 teaspoon instant coffee granules
- 2 teaspoons vanilla
- 1 cup whipped cream, optional
  Chocolate curls, optional

Preheat oven to 350°. Beat cream cheese, sugar and eggs in bowl until smooth. Blend in melted chocolate chips, cream, coffee granules and vanilla. Pour into pie shell. Bake 40 to 50 minutes or until set. (Center may be a bit soft, but it will firm as it cools.) Chill 3 to 4 hours. Serve garnished with whipped cream and chocolate curls, if desired.

Chocolate Layer Pie

Preparation Time: 1 hour, 10 minutes.

- 1 9-inch unbaked pastry shell
- ½ cup granulated sugar
- ¼ cup unsweetened cocoa
- ½ teaspoon vanilla
- 2 tablespoons cold coffee
- ¼ cup water
- 1 cup flour
- 1 cup granulated sugar
- ½ teaspoon ground cinnamon
- 1 teaspoon baking powder
- ½ cup chopped pecans
- ¼ cup butter, melted
- 1 egg, lightly beaten
- ½ cup milk
- ½ teaspoon vanilla

Preheat oven to 350°. Combine ½ cup sugar, cocoa, ½ teaspoon vanilla, coffee and water in bowl; pour into pie shell. Mix flour, 1 cup sugar, cinnamon, baking powder and pecans in bowl; stir in butter, egg, milk and vanilla. Pour over chocolate layer. Bake 40 to 50 minutes or until toothpick inserted in center comes out clean. Cool on rack.

Pumpkin Praline Pie

Preparation Time: 1 hour, 45 minutes.

  1 9-inch unbaked pastry shell
½ cup light brown sugar, packed
½ cup pecans
  2 tablespoons butter *or* margarine, softened
  2 eggs, beaten
  1 cup canned pumpkin
½ cup milk
½ cup sherry
½ teaspoon ground cinnamon
½ teaspoon ground ginger
¼ teaspoon ground cloves
¼ teaspoon ground allspice
   Dash salt
  1 cup whipped cream, optional

Preheat oven to 375°. Mix brown sugar, pecans and butter together in bowl; press lightly into bottom of pie shell. Mix remaining ingredients except whipped cream; pour into pie shell. Bake 45 minutes or until knife inserted in center comes out clean. Cool on rack. Garnish with whipped cream just before serving, if desired.

Pecan Pie

Preparation Time: 1 hour, 10 minutes.

  1 9-inch unbaked pastry shell
  3 eggs
½ cup granulated sugar
  1 cup dark corn syrup
⅛ teaspoon salt
  1 teaspoon vanilla
¼ cup butter *or* margarine, melted
  1 cup whole pecans

Preheat oven to 350°. Beat eggs in bowl; add sugar and syrup. Beat in salt, vanilla and butter. Spread pecans evenly in bottom of pie shell; add filling. Bake 50 to 60 minutes. Nuts will rise to top of pie to form crust. Cool on rack.

Custard Surprise Pie

This pie has no crust.

Makes 1 9-inch pie *or* 1 10-inch pie.
Preparation Time: 1 hour, 10 minutes.

1½ cups milk
  3 eggs, lightly beaten
¼ cup granulated sugar
½ cup flaked coconut
½ cup sliced almonds
  3 tablespoons butter *or* margarine, melted
⅓ cup biscuit mix
½ teaspoon vanilla
½ teaspoon almond extract
   Dash salt

Preheat oven to 350°. Mix all ingredients; beat until well blended. Pour into buttered 9-inch pie pan. Bake 45 to 55 minutes. Cool on rack.

Note: For 10-inch pie, prepare as above, using 2 cups milk, 4 eggs, ¾ cups granulated sugar, 1 cup coconut, 1 cup almonds, ¼ cup butter, ½ cup biscuit mix, 1 teaspoon vanilla, ½ teaspoon almond extract and dash of salt.

Governor's Palace Rum Pie

Preparation Time: 30 minutes plus chilling time.

  1 9-inch baked Chocolate Crumb Crust (Recipe on page 9)
  3 eggs
¾ cup granulated sugar
  1 tablespoon unflavored gelatin
½ cup cold water
½ cup milk
  1 teaspoon rum flavoring
  1 teaspoon vanilla
  1 cup whipping cream, whipped
  2 tablespoons grated sweet chocolate
  6 maraschino cherries, halved

Beat eggs in bowl until thick; stir in sugar. Soften gelatin in cold water in saucepan. Add egg mixture and milk; cook over low heat, stirring, 2 minutes or until gelatin is dissolved. Stir in rum and vanilla; cool until mixture mounds when dropped from spoon. Fold in whipped cream. Pour into crust. Chill until firm. Garnish with grated chocolate and cherries.

Hot Fudge Sundae Pie

Preparation Time: 1 hour, 15 minutes.

  1 9-inch unbaked pastry shell
  2 ounces unsweetened chocolate, melted
½ cup light brown sugar, packed
  1 cup granulated sugar
¼ cup butter
¼ teaspoon salt
  3 eggs, lightly beaten
½ cup milk
½ cup chopped walnuts
  1 teaspoon vanilla
   Vanilla ice cream, optional

Preheat oven to 350°. Mix chocolate and sugars in saucepan. Add butter; stir over low heat until well blended; remove from heat. Mix in salt, eggs, milk, nuts and vanilla. Pour into pie shell. Bake 55 to 60 minutes. Cool on rack. Top with scoops of vanilla ice cream, if desired.

Custard Pies

Lemon Lattice Pie

This lemon custard pie is topped with a lattice of sugar-cookie dough.

Preparation Time: 2 hours.

    1 9-inch unbaked pastry shell
    2 cups granulated sugar
    ¼ cup plus 2 tablespoons flour
    6 eggs, beaten
    ½ cup butter
    1 cup lemon juice
    2 teaspoons grated lemon rind
      Lattice

Mix sugar and flour in top of double boiler; beat in eggs, butter, lemon juice and lemon rind. Cook, stirring constantly, 12 to 15 minutes or until mixture thickens. Cool. Pour into pie shell; set aside. Prepare Lattice; weave into lattice design on top of custard-filled pie shell. Preheat oven to 350°. Bake 30 to 35 minutes until golden brown. Cool on rack.

Lattice

    1 cup flour
    ½ cup light brown sugar, packed
    1 teaspoon baking powder
    ¼ teaspoon ground nutmeg
    ¼ cup butter *or* margarine
    1 egg, lightly beaten
    1 tablespoon milk

Mix flour, sugar, baking powder and nutmeg in bowl; cut in butter until mixture resembles small peas. Stir in egg and milk. Knead slightly; form into ball. Chill 30 minutes. Roll dough into 11-inch circle on lightly floured surface; cut into strips.

Chocolate Pecan Pie

Preparation Time: 1 hour.

    1 9-inch unbaked pastry shell
    2 ounces unsweetened chocolate
    ¼ cup strong hot coffee
    2 tablespoons butter
    4 eggs, lightly beaten
    1 cup light corn syrup
    ½ cup granulated sugar
    1½ cups pecan halves
      Whipped cream, optional
      Pecan halves, optional

Preheat oven to 375°. Melt chocolate in coffee in saucepan; stir until smooth. Stir in butter. Cool. Beat eggs, corn syrup and sugar until fluffy; stir in chocolate mixture and nuts. Pour into pie shell. Bake 35 to 40 minutes. Cool on rack. Serve with dollops of whipped cream and additional pecan halves, if desired.

Kentucky Pecan Pie

Pecans marinated in bourbon for 1 hour give this pie punch.

Preparation Time: 2 hours, 10 minutes.

    1 9-inch unbaked pastry shell
    ¼ cup bourbon
    ½ teaspoon vanilla
    1 cup pecan halves
    2 tablespoons flour
    ½ cup light brown sugar, packed
    2 tablespoons milk
    2 tablespoons butter *or* margarine, melted
    1 cup dark corn syrup
    3 eggs, lightly beaten
    ¼ teaspoon salt

Preheat oven to 350°. Pour bourbon and vanilla over pecan halves; marinate 1 hour. Mix flour and sugar in bowl; stir in milk, butter, syrup, eggs and salt. Drain bourbon off pecans; discard bourbon. Scatter pecans on pie shell; pour egg mixture over nuts. Bake 50 to 60 minutes or until knife inserted in custard comes out clean. Cool on rack.

Pecan Chess Pie

Preparation Time: 1 hour, 15 minutes.

    1 9-inch unbaked pastry shell
    ½ cup butter *or* margarine
    1½ cups granulated sugar
    1 tablespoon cornmeal
    3 eggs, lightly beaten
    1 tablespoon lemon juice
    1 teaspoon vanilla
    1 cup pecan halves
    ½ cup toasted flaked coconut

Preheat oven to 350°. Melt butter in saucepan; stir in sugar, cornmeal, eggs, lemon juice and vanilla. Place nuts and coconut in bottom of pie shell. Top with egg mixture; bake 50 to 60 minutes or until knife inserted in custard comes out clean. Cool on rack.

Note: To toast flaked coconut, spread coconut on baking sheet; bake at 325° 10 minutes or until golden brown.

Pecan Pie, page 17

Refrigerator Pies

Frozen Chocolate-Almond Pie

Preparation Time: 15 minutes plus 3 hours to chill.

    1 9-inch Toasted Almond Crust, chilled (Recipe on page 9)
    1 quart chocolate ice cream, softened
    1 cup whipping cream, whipped
    1 teaspoon vanilla
    1 tablespoon rum flavoring
    ¼ cup toasted slivered almonds, to garnish

Quickly mix ice cream, whipped cream, vanilla and rum flavoring; spoon into crust. Freeze 1½ to 3 hours. Sprinkle with almonds before serving.

Variations

Chocolate Chip: Follow directions using 1 quart chocolate-chip ice cream; 1 cup whipping cream, whipped; and ¼ cup light creme de cacao. Drizzle ¼ cup chocolate syrup over pie before serving.

Peach: Follow directions using 1 quart peach ice cream; 1 cup whipping cream, whipped; and 1 tablespoon lemon juice. Garnish with 1 cup sliced fresh peaches.

Pistachio-Almond: Follow directions using 1 quart pistachio *or* macaroon ice cream; 1 cup whipping cream, whipped; and 1 teaspoon almond extract. Garnish with ½ cup toasted slivered almonds and 6 to 8 halved maraschino cherries.

Strawberry: Follow directions using 1 quart strawberry ice cream; 1 cup whipping cream, whipped; 2 tablespoons orange-flavored liqueur; and 1 cup sliced strawberries. Garnish with 8 to 10 whole strawberries.

Chocolate-Coconut Ice Cream Pie

This pie has no crust.

Preparation Time: 20 minutes plus 8 hours to freeze.

    2 ounces unsweetened chocolate
    2 tablespoons butter *or* margarine
    ⅔ cup confectioners' sugar
    2 tablespoons hot water
    1½ cups flaked coconut
    1½ quarts coffee ice cream *or* flavor of your choice, softened

Melt chocolate and butter in saucepan. Combine sugar and water in bowl; stir in chocolate. Blend in coconut. Press on bottom and up side of buttered 9-inch pie pan. Chill 1 hour. Fill with ice cream, smoothing evenly. Freeze overnight. Place in refrigerator 20 to 30 minutes before serving.

Strawberry Ice Cream Pie

Preparation Time: 45 minutes plus time to freeze.

    1½ cups flaked coconut
    1 tablespoon butter
    1½ cups sliced strawberries
    1 tablespoon orange-flavored liqueur
    1 quart vanilla ice cream, softened slightly
    8 to 12 whole strawberries, to garnish

Preheat oven to 325°. Spread coconut on baking sheet; toast 10 to 12 minutes until lightly browned. Cool. Butter 9-inch pie pan with 1 tablespoon butter. Press coconut onto bottom and up side of pan to form crust. Sprinkle sliced strawberries with orange liqueur; stir gently into softened ice cream. Spoon into crust; freeze. Garnish with whole berries before serving.

Unbaked Cheese Pie

Preparation Time: 20 minutes plus chilling time.

    1 9-inch baked pastry shell
    4 3-ounce packages cream cheese, softened
    ½ cup confectioners' sugar
    1 teaspoon grated lemon rind
    2 tablespoons lemon juice
    2 tablespoons cream
    ½ cup whipping cream, whipped

Beat cheese, sugar, lemon rind, lemon juice and cream in bowl until fluffy. Fold whipped cream into cheese mixture; pour into pie shell. Chill.

Note: Top with fresh fruit of your choice and a fruit glaze, if desired.

* * *

Melt chocolate in a heavy saucepan over low heat. Remove from the heat when the chocolate is partially melted; the heat of the pan will finish the melting process. Chocolate also can be melted in the top of a double boiler placed over hot, *not* boiling, water.

Peach-Berry Pie

Peach-Berry Pie is berry delicious—winter or summer.

Preparation Time: 45 minutes plus 2 hours to chill.

- **1 9-inch baked pastry shell**
- **¼ cup granulated sugar**
- **2 tablespoons cornstarch**
- **2 cups strawberries, washed, hulled and crushed**
- **2 tablespoons lemon juice**
- **3 cups fresh *or* canned peach slices, drained**
- **1 cup strawberries, washed, hulled and halved**

Mix sugar, cornstarch, crushed strawberries and lemon juice in saucepan; cook over medium heat, stirring constantly, until thickened and clear. Cool. Place peach slices and halved strawberries in pie shell in attractive design. Pour strawberry glaze over fruit. Chill 2 hours.

Peaches 'n' Cream Pie

Preparation Time: 2 hours plus time to chill.

- **1 9-inch baked pastry shell**
- **1½ cups chopped peaches**
- **¾ cup granulated sugar**
- **⅛ teaspoon salt**
- **1 tablespoon lemon juice**
- **1 tablespoon unflavored gelatin**
- **¼ cup cold water**
- **½ cup boiling water**
- **1 cup whipped cream, whipped, *or* nondairy whipped topping**

Mix peaches with sugar, salt and lemon juice in bowl. Let stand 30 minutes. Soften gelatin in cold water; add boiling water. Cool. Add gelatin mixture to peach mixture. Chill until mixture mounds when dropped from spoon. Fold in whipped cream; pour into pie shell. Refrigerate until set.

Buttercream Pie

Preparation Time: 1 hour plus 12 hours to chill.

- **2 cups vanilla cookie crumbs**
- **1 cup butter, softened**
- **2 cups confectioners' sugar**
- **4 eggs**
- **1 teaspoon vanilla**
- **½ teaspoon almond extract**
- **½ cup slivered almonds**
- **½ cup chopped maraschino cherries**
- **1 cup whipping cream, whipped**
- **10 to 12 whole maraschino cherries**

Butter 10-inch pie plate; press 1 cup crumbs firmly on bottom. Cream butter and sugar in large mixing bowl; add eggs, 1 at a time, beating constantly until well blended. Add flavorings; stir in almonds. Spoon evenly over crumb crust. Sprinkle ¾ cup crumbs over buttercream mixture. Fold chopped cherries into whipped cream; spoon over crumb layer. Sprinkle remaining ¼ cup crumbs over cream. Garnish with whole cherries. Chill 12 hours before serving.

Note: Pie can be wrapped tightly and frozen for future use. Place in refrigerator 2 hours before serving.

Frozen Lemon Pie

Preparation Time: 30 minutes plus freezing time.

- **1 9-inch baked pastry shell**
- **3 eggs, separated**
- **½ cup granulated sugar**
  Dash salt
- **1 teaspoon grated lemon rind**
- **¼ cup lemon juice**
- **¼ cup granulated sugar**
- **1 cup whipping cream, whipped**
  Thin lemon peel slivers, optional

Beat egg yolks, ½ cup sugar, salt, lemon rind and juice in saucepan. Cook, whisking constantly until thick. Cool. Beat egg whites until soft peaks form; gradually add ¼ cup sugar, beating until stiff peaks form. Fold into cooled lemon mixture. Fold in whipped cream; pour into pie shell. Garnish with lemon peel slivers, if desired; freeze. Remove from freezer to refrigerator 20 to 30 minutes before serving.

Grasshopper Pie

Preparation Time: 1 hour, 20 minutes plus time to freeze.

- **1 9-inch baked Chocolate Crumb Crust (Recipe on page 9)**
- **30 large marshmallows**
- **½ cup milk**
- **¼ cup green creme de menthe**
- **2 tablespoons white creme de cacao**
- **1 cup whipping cream, whipped**

Melt marshmallows in milk in large saucepan. Remove from heat; stir in liqueurs. Cool 1 hour. Fold in whipped cream; pour into crust. Freeze. Serve frozen.

Chiffon Pies

Basic Chiffon Pie

Preparation Time: 1 hour, 10 minutes plus chilling time.

    1 9-inch baked crumb crust
    4 eggs, separated
 1½ cups milk
    1 tablespoon unflavored gelatin
 ½ cup granulated sugar
 ¼ teaspoon salt
 ½ cup whipping cream, whipped, optional

Beat egg yolks, milk, gelatin, sugar and salt in heavy saucepan. Cook and stir over low heat until thickened. Chill until mixture mounds when dropped from spoon. Beat egg whites to peaks; fold into gelatin mixture. For a richer pie, fold in whipped cream. Spoon filling into crust. Chill several hours.

Variations

Coffee Chiffon: Substitute 1½ cups strong coffee for milk.

Chocolate Chiffon: Add 6 tablespoons cocoa *or* 2 ounces melted unsweetened chocolate and 1 tablespoon orange liqueur after removing filling mixture from heat.

Airy-Berry Pie

Pale pink and lusciously light, this pie uses strawberries in a different way.

Preparation Time: 1 hour plus chilling time.

    1 9-inch baked pastry shell
    1 tablespoon unflavored gelatin
 ½ cup cold water
    1 10-ounce package frozen strawberries, thawed
    1 tablespoon lemon juice
       Dash salt
    2 egg whites, room tempeature
    2 tablespoons granulated sugar
 ½ cup whipping cream, whipped
    6 whole strawberries, for garnish

Soften gelatin in cold water; dissolve over low heat; remove from heat. Add strawberries, lemon juice and salt. Refrigerate until mixture mounds slightly when dropped from spoon. Beat egg whites until soft peaks form. Gradually add sugar; beat until stiff peaks form. Fold whipped cream and egg whites into strawberry mixture. Pour into pie shell. Chill. Garnish with whole strawberries.

"Mile High" Lemon Chiffon Pie

Preparation Time: 1 hour plus chilling time.

    1 9-inch baked pastry shell
    8 egg yolks, lightly beaten
    1 cup granulated sugar
    1 tablespoon unflavored gelatin
 ½ cup water
    1 tablespoon grated lemon rind
 ½ cup lemon juice
 ¼ teaspoon salt
    8 egg whites, room temperature
 ½ cup granulated sugar

Mix egg yolks, 1 cup sugar, gelatin, water, lemon rind, lemon juice and salt in heavy saucepan. Cook over medium heat, stirring constantly, until mixture starts to thicken and just comes to a boil. Chill, stirring occasionally, until mixture mounds when dropped from spoon. Beat egg whites until frothy; add ½ cup sugar, 1 tablespoon at a time, beating until stiff, glossy peaks form. Fold into lemon mixture. Pour into pie shell. Refrigerate several hours until set.

Lime Chiffon Pie

Frozen limeade is the secret to this pie.

Preparation Time: 1 hour, 10 minutes plus chilling time.

    1 9-inch baked pastry shell *or* Chocolate Crumb Crust (Recipe on page 9)
    1 tablespoon unflavored gelatin
 ½ cup cold water
    3 egg yolks, well beaten
       Dash salt
    1 6-ounce can frozen limeade concentrate, thawed, strained
    3 egg whites, room temperature
 ¼ cup granulated sugar
 ½ cup whipping cream, whipped

Soften gelatin in water in top of double boiler. Add egg yolks and salt. Cook over low heat until mixture thickens slightly, whisking constantly. Remove from heat, add limeade concentrate, and stir until dissolved. Chill until mixture mounds when dropped from spoon. Beat egg whites until soft peaks form. Gradually add sugar, beating until stiff peaks form. Gently fold egg whites and whipped cream into gelatin mixture. Spoon into pie shell; chill until firm.

Lime Chiffon Pie, this page

Chiffon Pies

Blueberry Eggnog Pie

This chiffon custard pie is topped with sugared whole blueberries.

Preparation Time: 1 hour, 10 minutes plus chilling time.

  1 9-inch baked pastry shell
  ¼ cup granulated sugar
  1 tablespoon unflavored gelatin
    Dash salt
  3 egg yolks, beaten
  1½ cups milk
  1 teaspoon vanilla
  3 egg whites, room temperature
  ¼ cup granulated sugar
  ½ cup whipping cream, whipped
  ⅛ teaspoon ground nutmeg
  1 to 2 cups blueberries, washed and drained
  ¼ cup granulated sugar

Combine ¼ cup sugar, gelatin and salt in top of double boiler; add egg yolks and milk. Cook, stirring over low heat until mixture thickens slightly; remove from heat. Add vanilla. Chill, stirring occasionally, until mixture mounds when dropped from spoon. Beat egg whites until soft peaks form. Add ¼ cup sugar gradually; beat until stiff peaks form. Beat gelatin mixture until smooth; fold in egg whites and whipped cream. Pour into pie shell; sprinkle with nutmeg. Chill until firm. Combine blueberries and ¼ cup sugar 10 minutes before serving. Top each piece of pie with spoonful of berries.

Chocolate-Cinnamon Cream Pie

Chocolate and cinnamon is a good combination in this pie.

Preparation Time: 1 hour, 15 minutes plus 3 to 4 hours to chill.

  1 9-inch baked Chocolate Crumb Crust (Recipe on page 9)
  3 eggs, separated
  1⅓ cups milk
  ½ cup granulated sugar
  1 teaspoon ground cinnamon
    Dash salt
  1 tablespoon unflavored gelatin
  1 teaspoon vanilla
  ½ cup whipping cream, whipped
  ½ cup grated sweet chocolate, for garnish, optional

Mix egg yolks, milk, sugar, cinnamon, salt and gelatin in saucepan. Cook over low heat, stirring with whisk, until mixture thickens. Remove from heat; stir in vanilla. Chill until mixture mounds when dropped from spoon. Beat with whisk until smooth. Fold in whipped cream. Beat egg whites until stiff peaks form; gently fold into gelatin mixture. Spoon into crust. Chill until set, 3 to 4 hours. Garnish with grated chocolate just before serving, if desired.

Black Bottom Pie

Preparation Time: 1 hour, 20 minutes plus 1 hour to chill.

  1 9-inch baked Chocolate Crumb Crust (Recipe on page 9)
  1½ cups granulated sugar
  2 tablespoons flour
    Dash salt
  1½ cups milk
  3 eggs, separated
  2 ounces unsweetened chocolate, melted
  1 teaspoon vanilla
  1 tablespoon unflavored gelatin
  ¼ cup water
  ¼ teaspoon cream of tartar
  ¼ cup granulated sugar
  2 teaspoons vanilla
  1 teaspoon rum flavoring
    Topping
  3 tablespoons grated semisweet chocolate, for garnish, optional

Mix 1½ cups sugar, flour, salt, milk and egg yolks in saucepan. Cook, stirring constantly, over medium heat until mixture boils. Put 1 cup of mixture in small bowl; stir in chocolate and 1 teaspoon vanilla. Spread on bottom of crust. Soften gelatin in water; stir into remaining custard; chill until mixture thickens. Beat egg whites and cream of tartar until foamy. Add ¼ cup sugar gradually; beat until mixture forms stiff peaks. Beat in 2 teaspoons vanilla and rum flavoring. Fold beaten egg whites into cooled custard. Pour over chocolate layer; chill. Prepare Topping at serving time; spread over cooled pie. Garnish with grated chocolate, if desired.

Topping

  1 cup whipping cream
  2 tablespoons granulated sugar
  ½ teaspoon vanilla

Whip cream and sugar until thick. Stir in vanilla.

Cranberry Ribbon Pie

Preparation Time: 1 hour, 30 minutes plus 2 to 3 hours to chill.

    1 9-inch baked pastry shell
    1 cup whole berry cranberry sauce
    ¼ cup orange juice
    1 tablespoon cornstarch
    2 egg yolks, lightly beaten
    ⅓ cup granulated sugar
    1 tablespoon unflavored gelatin
      Dash salt
    1 cup milk
    1 teaspoon rum flavoring or vanilla
    2 egg whites, room temperature
    ¼ teaspoon cream of tartar
    ¼ cup granulated sugar
    ½ cup whipping cream, whipped
      Frosted Cranberries

Combine cranberry sauce, orange juice and cornstarch in saucepan; cook 3 to 4 minutes over medium heat until thickened and clear. Cool. Spread in bottom of pie shell; set aside. Mix egg yolks, ⅓ cup sugar, gelatin, salt, milk and flavoring in saucepan; cook over medium heat, stirring constantly, until mixture comes to boil; remove from heat. Chill until mixture mounds when dropped from spoon. Beat whites and cream of tartar until foamy; add ¼ cup sugar gradually, beating until stiff, glossy peaks form. Fold whipped cream and egg whites into gelatin mixture. Pour gelatin mixture into pie shell over cranberry mixture. Refrigerate 2 to 3 hours or until set. Arrange Frosted Cranberries in clusters on top of pie before serving.

Frosted Cranberries

    12 to 15 fresh cranberries
    ½ cup granulated sugar

Moisten each cranberry in water; roll in sugar. Place on paper towel to dry.

Strawberry Wine Pie

Preparation Time: 1 hour plus 4 to 5 hours to chill.

    1 9-inch baked pastry shell
    4 eggs, separated
    ½ cup Rhine wine
    ½ cup granulated sugar
      Dash salt
    1 tablespoon unflavored gelatin
    2 tablespoons granulated sugar
    1 cup whipping cream
    ¼ teaspoon almond extract
    8 to 10 whole strawberries, for garnish

Beat egg yolks, wine, ½ cup sugar and salt in saucepan with fork until blended. Sprinkle gelatin over egg mixture; cook over low heat, stirring constantly, until gelatin is dissolved and mixture thickens, about 5 to 7 minutes. Remove from heat. Beat egg whites until foamy; gradually beat in 2 tablespoons sugar until stiff peaks form. Set aside. Beat whipping cream and almond extract until stiff peaks form. Gently fold whipped cream and egg whites into gelatin mixture. Pour into pie shell; refrigerate 4 to 5 hours. Garnish with strawberries.

Rhubarb Chiffon Pie

Preparation Time: 1 hour, 45 minutes.

    1 9-inch baked pastry shell
    4 cups ½-inch rhubarb pieces
    1 cup granulated sugar
    2 tablespoons water
    1 tablespoon unflavored gelatin
    1 tablespoon orange juice concentrate
    3 eggs, separated
    2 tablespoons granulated sugar
    1 cup whipping cream
    ½ teaspoon vanilla
    6 to 8 whole strawberries, for garnish

Combine rhubarb, 1 cup sugar and water in saucepan. Cook over medium heat until sugar dissolves, about 5 minutes. Cover; cook over low heat 10 minutes until rhubarb is tender. Drain, reserving juice. Return juice to saucepan; boil until reduced by one half. Pour over rhubarb. Sprinkle gelatin over orange juice concentrate in saucepan. Add egg yolks; cook, beating well, over low heat until gelatin dissolves, about 8 minutes. Stir in rhubarb; chill until mixture thickens, about 25 minutes. Beat egg whites in large bowl until foamy; gradually add 2 tablespoons sugar; beat until stiff peaks form. Gently fold into rhubarb mixture. Spoon into pie shell; refrigerate 2 hours. Just before serving, whip cream with vanilla until stiff; spoon onto pie. Garnish with strawberries.

* * *

When whipping cream, thoroughly chill the bowl and beaters so the cream will whip to a higher volume.

Fruit Pies

Plum Pie

Preparation Time: 1 hour, 20 minutes.

    Pastry for 9-inch double piecrust
4 cups sliced plums
1 tablespoon lemon juice
½ teaspoon almond extract
¼ cup butter *or* **margarine**
¼ cup flour
1½ cups granulated sugar

Preheat oven to 450°. Roll one half of pastry; line 9-inch pie pan. Gently toss plums with lemon juice and almond extract; place in pie shell. Dot with butter. Combine flour and sugar; sprinkle over fruit. Roll remaining pastry to fit over pie; seal edges; cut slits in top to vent steam. Bake 35 to 45 minutes until brown and bubbly. Cool on rack.

Apple-Nut Cobbler Pie

This delicious old-fashioned cobbler has pie on the bottom and cake on the top. Serve it with cream.

Preparation Time: 1 hour, 20 minutes.

    Pastry for 9-inch piecrust
½ cup granulated sugar
½ teaspoon ground cinnamon
¼ teaspoon ground nutmeg
¾ cup chopped walnuts
4 cups pared, thinly sliced tart apples
1 cup flour
1 cup granulated sugar
1 teaspoon baking powder
¼ teaspoon salt
1 egg, beaten
½ cup milk
⅓ cup butter, melted
1 cup cream

Preheat oven to 450°. Butter a 2-quart round casserole; roll pastry and line bottom of casserole. Prick pastry with tines of fork; bake 5 minutes. Reduce heat to 325°. Mix ½ cup sugar, cinnamon, nutmeg and ½ of walnuts. Place apples on pastry; sprinkle with sugar mixture. Mix flour, 1 cup sugar, baking powder and salt in bowl; mix in egg, milk and butter until smooth. Pour over apples; sprinkle with remaining walnuts. Bake 50 to 55 minutes. Serve warm with cream.

French Apple Pie

Preparation Time: 1 hour, 30 minutes.

  1½ cups flour
  6 tablespoons butter
  ¼ teaspoon salt
  5 to 6 cups pared, chopped apples
  1 tablespoon lemon juice
  3 tablespoons flour
  ¾ cup granulated sugar
  1 teaspoon ground cinnamon
  ¼ teaspoon salt
  ½ cup butter, softened
  ½ cup light brown sugar, packed
  1 cup flour

Preheat oven to 375°. Combine 1½ cups flour, 6 tablespoons butter and ¼ teaspoon salt in bowl. Pat in bottom and up side of 9- or 10-inch pie pan. Combine apples, lemon juice, 3 tablespoons flour, ¾ cup sugar, cinnamon and ¼ teaspoon salt; spoon into piecrust. Cream ½ cup butter with brown sugar until fluffy. Cut in 1 cup flour until mixture is crumbly; sprinkle evenly over apples. Bake 55 minutes. Cool on rack.

Fruit Streusel Pie

Here is a basic recipe for fruit pie with streusel topping.

Preparation Time: 1 hour.

  1 9-inch unbaked pastry shell
  1 cup dairy sour cream
  2 tablespoons flour
  1 cup granulated sugar
  Dash salt
  1 egg, beaten
  2 cups peeled and sliced peaches, pears *or* **apples** *or* **blueberries** *or* **hulled strawberries**
  ⅓ cup flour
  ½ cup granulated sugar
  ¼ cup butter, melted
  1 teaspon grated lemon rind, optional

Preheat oven to 375°. Combine sour cream, 2 tablespoons flour, 1 cup sugar, salt, egg and fruit in bowl; pour into pie shell. Bake 40 minutes. Combine ⅓ cup flour, ½ cup sugar, butter and lemon rind, if desired. Sprinkle mixture over hot pie. Bake 10 minutes. Cool on rack.

Plum Pie, this page
Apple Pie, page 29

Fruit Pies

Blueberry Pie

Preparation Time: 1 hour.

1 9-inch baked butter pastry shell
1 cup granulated sugar
2 tablespoons cornstarch
4 cups blueberries, washed and drained
1 tablespoon water
2 teaspoons lemon juice
1 teaspoon grated lemon rind
1 tablespoon granulated sugar
½ cup dairy sour cream

Mix 1 cup sugar, cornstarch, 2 cups blueberries and water in saucepan. Heat to boiling; cook, stirring constantly, until thickened and clear. Remove from heat. Stir in lemon juice, lemon rind and remaining blueberries. Cool; spread in pie shell. Beat 1 tablespoon sugar into sour cream; pour over cooled pie.

Brandied Apple Pie

Preparation Time: 1 hour, 10 minutes.

1 9-inch unbaked pastry shell
2 eggs, lightly beaten
1½ cups applesauce
½ cup granulated sugar
1 tablespoon brandy
2 tablespoons orange marmalade
2 cups peeled, thick tart apple slices
2 tablespoons lemon juice
Dash ground nutmeg
2 tablespoons light brown sugar
2 tablespoons butter, melted

Preheat oven to 375°. Beat eggs, applesauce, ½ cup sugar, brandy and marmalade in separate bowl. Pour into pie shell. Toss apple slices and lemon juice in bowl; arrange in circles on top of egg mixture. Mix nutmeg, brown sugar and butter; sprinkle over apples. Bake 40 to 45 minutes or until knife inserted in center comes out clean and apples are glazed. Cool on rack.

Cherry Pie

Preparation Time: 1 hour, 35 minutes.

1 9-inch unbaked pastry shell *or* **1** 9-inch unbaked double pastry crust
4 cups pitted tart cherries
1½ cups granulated sugar
3 tablespoons tapioca
1 teaspoon lemon juice
½ teaspoon almond extract
Dash salt
2 tablespoons butter

Preheat oven to 425°. Combine cherries, sugar, tapioca, lemon juice, almond extract and salt in bowl; set aside 30 minutes. Pour into pie shell. Dot with butter. Top with foil *or* remaining top piecrust (if using double crust). Cut 3 slits to vent steam. Bake 40 to 45 minutes. Cool on rack.

Cream Cheese and Date Pie

Cream cheese and dates, long a favorite for sandwiches, combine in a delicious pie.

Preparation Time: 1 hour, 30 minutes.

1 9-inch unbaked pastry shell
1 cup chopped dates
2 teaspoons grated orange rind
½ cup orange juice
1 8-ounce package cream cheese, softened
½ cup granulated sugar
Dash salt
2 eggs, lightly beaten
⅓ cup milk
½ teaspoon vanilla
Dash ground nutmeg

Preheat oven to 400°. Simmer dates, orange rind and orange juice in saucepan 3 to 4 minutes, stirring occasionally. Cool. Beat cream cheese, sugar, salt, eggs, milk and vanilla in bowl until smooth; fold in date mixture. Pour into pie shell; sprinkle with nutmeg. Bake 10 minutes; reduce heat to 325°. Bake 20 to 30 minutes. Cool on rack.

Deep Dish Strawberry-Rhubarb Pie

Strawberries and rhubarb combine in a deep dish pie in which the crust is on top.

Preparation Time: 1 hour, 15 minutes.

Pastry for 9-inch single piecrust
3 cups ½-inch rhubarb pieces
2 cups sliced strawberries
1 tablespoon lemon juice
1½ cups granulated sugar
3 tablespoons tapioca
½ teaspoon vanilla
2 tablespoons butter *or* margarine
1 tablespoon granulated sugar

Preheat oven to 400°. Place fruits and lemon juice in 8-inch square baking dish. Combine 1½ cups sugar and tapioca; toss gently with fruit. Sprinkle with vanilla and dot with butter. Roll pastry to 9-inch square and place over fruit. Crimp at edge of pan to seal; cut 3 slits to vent steam. Sprinkle with 1 tablespoon sugar. Bake 45 to 50 minutes until crust is golden brown. Cool on rack.

Fresh Peach Pie

Preparation Time: 1 hour, 15 minutes plus 1 hour to chill.

    1 9-inch baked pastry shell
    4 cups peeled, pitted and sliced peaches
    1 tablespoon lemon juice
    1 cup granulated sugar
      Water
    3 tablespoons cornstarch
    ⅛ teaspoon salt
    2 teaspoons butter
      Whipped cream or frozen topping

Sprinkle peaches with lemon juice and sugar; cover and let stand 1 hour. Drain; measure peach liquid; add water to make 1 cup. Blend peach liquid and cornstarch in saucepan until smooth; bring to boil, stirring constantly, until thick and clear, about 2 to 3 minutes. Remove from heat. Add salt and butter; cool. Toss peaches with sauce; spoon into pie shell. Chill 1 hour. Top with whipped cream before serving.

Fresh Strawberry Pie

This pie is pretty as a picture.

Preparation Time: 40 minutes plus chilling time.

    1 9-inch graham cracker crust or baked pastry shell
    2 pints strawberries, washed and hulled
    1 cup granulated sugar
    3 tablespoons cornstarch
    2 tablespoons lemon juice
      Whipped cream, optional

Crush 1 pint strawberries in saucepan with fork. Combine sugar with cornstarch and lemon juice; stir into strawberries. Cook over moderate heat, stirring, until clear and thickened; cool. Halve remaining pint strawberries; fold into mixture. Pour into crust. Chill thoroughly. Serve with whipped cream, if desired.

Scandinavian Apricot Flan

Preparation Time: 1 hour, 30 minutes.

    1½ cups pumpernickel crumbs
    ½ cup ground walnuts
    ⅓ cup granulated sugar
    1 teaspoon grated lemon rind
    ½ teaspoon ground cinnamon
    ⅛ teaspoon ground cloves
    ¼ cup butter, melted
    ¼ cup burgundy
    2 16-ounce cans apricot halves, drained
    ½ cup apricot preserves
    1 teaspoon lemon juice
    1 cup whipping cream, whipped

Preheat oven to 350°. Combine crumbs, walnuts, sugar, lemon rind, cinnamon and cloves in bowl. Add butter to crumb mixture; mix well. Stir in burgundy. Press on bottom and up the side of 9-inch flan or pie pan. Bake 20 to 30 minutes. Cool. Arrange apricots on crust. Mix preserves with lemon juice; pour over fruit. Top with whipped cream.

Apple Pie

Makes 6 servings.
Preparation Time: 1 hour, 15 minutes.

    1 9-inch double piecrust (Recipe on page 6)
    6 cups peeled and sliced baking apples
    ¼ cup light brown sugar
    ¼ cup granulated sugar
    2 tablespoons flour
    1 teaspoon cinnamon
    ½ teaspoon nutmeg
    2 tablespoons butter
      Milk
      Sugar

Preheat oven to 425°. Combine apples, sugars, flour and spices; toss gently. Spoon into bottom crust. Dot with butter. Place top crust over filling; seal edges and flute (see page 4). Brush with milk and sprinkle with sugar. Cut slits in crust to allow steam to escape. Bake at 425° for 35 to 40 minutes or until golden. Cool on rack.

Cherry-Raspberry Pie

Makes 6 servings.
Preparation Time: 1 hour, 30 minutes.

    1 9-inch double piecrust (Recipe on page 6)
    3 cups pitted red tart cherries, fresh or canned
    1 pint fresh raspberries or 1 10-ounce package
      frozen raspberries, thawed and drained
    1 cup granulated sugar
    ¼ cup flour
    2 tablespoons butter
    1 egg yolk
    2 tablespoons water
      Granulated sugar

Preheat oven to 425°. Combine cherries, raspberries, sugar and flour in a large bowl; toss gently. Spoon into bottom crust; dot with butter. Prepare lattice top crust (see page 4) and place on top of filling. Mix egg yolk and water; brush over lattice. Sprinkle with sugar. Bake 30 to 35 minutes or until crust is golden. Cool on rack.

Meringue Shells & Pies

Almond Meringue Pie Shell

Makes 1 9-inch crust *or* 1 10-inch crust.
Preparation Time: 1 hour, 20 minutes.

  3 egg whites, room temperature
⅛ teaspoon salt
⅛ teaspoon cream of tartar
½ cup granulated sugar
½ teaspoon vanilla
½ teaspoon almond extract
½ cup finely chopped almonds

Preheat oven to 300°. Beat egg whites in bowl until foamy; beat in salt and cream of tartar. Gradually add sugar, 1 tablespoon at a time. Add flavorings; beat until stiff peaks form. Fold in nuts. Spread into 9-inch pie pan; spread evenly with back of spoon. Bake 55 to 60 minutes. Cool before filling.

Note: For 10-inch crust, prepare as above, using 4 egg whites, ⅛ teaspoon salt, ⅛ teaspoon cream of tartar, ¾ cup granulated sugar, ½ teaspoon vanilla, ½ teaspoon almond extract and ½ cup finely chopped almonds.

Chocolate Meringue Tart Shells

Makes 12 to 16.
Preparation Time: 1 hour.

  3 egg whites, room temperature
  Pinch cream of tartar
½ cup granulated sugar
½ cup confectioners' sugar
  1 tablespoon unsweetened cocoa

Preheat oven to 300°. Beat egg whites in clean, dry bowl with cream of tartar until soft peaks form. Beat in granulated sugar, 2 tablespoons at a time, until very stiff peaks form. Combine confectioners' sugar with cocoa in bowl; fold into meringue. Mound meringue ½-inch deep in 2¼-inch circles or 3 x 1½-inch ovals on ungreased baking sheets, mounding slightly along rims. Bake 30 minutes. Cool on racks.

Note: These are good filled with Chocolate Mousse (Recipe on page 40).

Meringue Nests

Makes 12 to 16.
Preparation Time: 1 hour, 15 minutes plus cooling time.

  4 egg whites, room temperature
¼ teaspoon cream of tartar
⅛ teaspoon salt
  1 teaspoon vanilla
  1 cup granulated sugar

Preheat oven to 275°. Beat egg whites in bowl until foamy. Add cream of tartar and salt; beat until stiff. Add vanilla. Beat in sugar, 1 tablespoon at a time, until glossy and stiff. Drop by tablespoonfuls onto ungreased baking sheets to form 12 to 16 mounds. Hollow out centers with back of spoon to form nests. Place in oven; reduce heat to 250°. Bake 45 minutes or until dry. Turn off oven; cool in oven.

Note: Meringues will keep in airtight container up to 2 weeks. Fill as desired. Quick Lemon Filling (Recipe on page 40) is good.

Meringue Shells

Makes 6 to 8.
Preparation Time: 1 hour, 30 minutes.

  3 egg whites, room temperature
½ teaspoon cream of tartar
⅛ teaspoon salt
¾ cup granulated sugar
  1 cup chopped nuts, optional

Preheat oven to 275°. Beat egg whites in bowl until foamy. Add cream of tartar and salt. Beat, adding sugar 2 tablespoons at a time, until very stiff peaks form. Fold in nuts, if desired. Cover baking sheets with brown paper. Divide meringue on baking sheets into 6 to 8 3-inch circles. Bake 1 hour. Cool on rack. Store in airtight containers.

Note: Fill meringues with 2 10-ounce packages frozen raspberries *or* sliced strawberries, thawed, topped with ice cream, whipped cream, Mocha Cream (Recipe on page 40) *or* Creme Café (Recipe on page 40).

Meringue Shells & Pies

Pecan Crumb-Meringue Shell

Makes 1 9-inch shell.
Preparation Time: 1 hour.

>   1 cup graham cracker crumbs
>   ¾ cup chopped pecans
>   4 egg whites, room temperature
>   Dash salt
>   1 teaspoon vanilla
>   1 cup granulated sugar

Preheat oven to 350°. Mix crumbs and nuts in bowl. Beat egg whites in separate bowl with salt and vanilla until foamy; gradually beat in sugar, 2 tablespoons at a time, until stiff peaks form. Fold into crumb-nut mixture. Pour into 9-inch pie pan, shaping with back of spoon. Bake 30 to 40 minutes or until lightly browned. Cool.

Note: Good filled with butter pecan *or* chocolate-mint ice cream, topped with hot fudge sauce.

Butterscotch Almond Pie

Preparation Time: 50 minutes.

>   1 deep 9-inch baked pastry shell
>   ¼ cup flour
>   1 cup light brown sugar, packed
>   ¼ teaspoon salt
>   2 cups milk
>   3 eggs, separated
>   1 teaspoon vanilla
>   ½ teaspoon almond extract
>   3 tablespoons butter
>   ½ cup slivered almonds, toasted
>   ½ teaspoon cream of tartar
>   2 tablespoons granulated sugar

Preheat oven to 350°. Mix flour, brown sugar and salt in saucepan. Add milk and beaten egg yolks; cook over low heat, stirring constantly, until thickened. Remove from heat; stir in flavorings and butter. Cool slightly; pour into pie shell. Sprinkle with almonds. Beat whites until foamy; sprinkle with cream of tartar; gradually beat in sugar until stiff, shiny peaks form. Spread meringue on top of pie, being sure it touches crust all around. Bake 18 minutes or until browned.

Baked Alaska Pie

Here are the basic directions for this delicious and showy dessert. Create your own version by combining your favorite fruits, ice cream flavors and sauces.

Preparation Time: 45 minutes plus 3 to 4 hours to freeze.

>   1 9-inch baked pastry shell *or* crumb crust, chilled
>   1 teaspoon fruit-flavored liqueur, optional
>   1 cup hulled strawberries, raspberries, pitted cherries, sliced bananas, blueberries *or* pitted, peeled and sliced peaches *or* apricots, sweetened to taste
>   1 quart ice cream *or* 1 pint each of 3 compatible flavors, slightly softened
>   Quick Chocolate Sauce (Recipe on page 45), optional

Pour liqueur over fruit in bowl; marinate 15 minutes. Drain and spoon fruit into pie shell. Spoon ice cream over fruit. (If using 3 flavors, spread in 3 layers.) Freeze until solid, 3 to 4 hours. Remove pie from freezer; frost with Meringue, making sure to cover ice cream to edge of pie shell. Return to freezer until serving time. To serve, preheat oven to 450°. Place pie directly from freezer into oven. Bake 3 to 5 minutes or until meringue is lightly browned. Serve immediately with Quick Chocolate Sauce, if desired.

Meringue

>   3 egg whites, room temperature
>   ⅛ teaspoon cream of tartar
>   ¼ cup granulated sugar

Beat whites in bowl until foamy. Add cream of tartar and sugar, 1 tablespoon at a time, beating constantly until stiff, shiny peaks form.

Variations

Chocolate-Banana: Use chocolate crumb crust; sliced bananas; chocolate, vanilla and butter almond ice creams; and hot fudge sauce.

Fruit Medley: Use pastry shell, strawberries, peach ice cream, and raspberry sauce.

Apricot: Use graham cracker crust, drained canned apricots, and pistachio ice cream. A sauce is not necessary.

Tropical: Use coconut crust, pineapple tidbits, vanilla ice cream, and orange sauce.

Lemon Meringue Pie

Preparation Time: 45 minutes.

    1 9-inch baked pastry shell
    1 cup granulated sugar
    6 tablespoons cornstarch
    1½ cups water
    ½ cup lemon juice
    2 teapoons grated lemon rind
    4 egg yolks, lightly beaten
    3 tablespoons butter
      Meringue

Preheat oven to 450°. Mix sugar and cornstarch in saucepan; add water, lemon juice, lemon rind and egg yolks. Cook over low heat, whisking constantly, until mixture thickens and clears; remove from heat. Add butter; whisk gently until butter melts and mixture cools slightly. Pour into pie shell. Prepare Meringue and spread onto filling, making sure to cover filling to edge of crust. Bake 8 to 10 minutes until lightly browned.

Meringue

    4 egg whites, room temperature
    ½ teaspoon cream of tartar
    ¼ cup granulated sugar

Beat egg whites in bowl until foamy. Add cream of tartar and sugar, 1 tablespoon at a time, until stiff peaks form and mixture is glossy.

Peanut Butter Meringue Pie

Preparation Time: 40 minutes.

    1 9-inch baked pastry shell
    ¾ cup granulated sugar
    3 tablespoons flour
    ¼ teaspoon salt
    3 cups milk
    3 eggs, separated
    ½ cup peanut butter
    1 teaspoon vanilla
    6 tablespoons granulated sugar

Preheat oven to 400°. Combine ¾ cup sugar, flour and salt in saucepan; mix in milk and lightly beaten egg yolks. Cook over low heat, stirring constantly with whisk. Bring to boil; boil gently 1 minute or until mixture coats back of spoon. Remove from heat; stir in peanut butter and vanilla. Pour into pie shell; set aside. Beat room temperature egg whites in bowl until foamy. Gradually add sugar, 2 tablespoons at a time, beating until stiff peaks form. Spread over filling, making sure meringue touches crust all around. Bake 6 to 8 minutes or until meringue is lightly browned. Cool on rack.

Strawberry Meringue Pie

Preparation Time: 1 hour, 15 minutes plus time to chill.

    1 9-inch baked Almond Meringue Pie Shell (Recipe on page 31)
    1 quart strawberries, washed and hulled
    ½ cup granulated sugar
    1 tablespoon lemon juice
    2 tablespoons unflavored gelatin
    ¼ cup orange juice
    1 cup whipping cream, whipped

Crush all but 10 strawberries in bowl; sprinkle with sugar and lemon juice. Sprinkle gelatin over orange juice in saucepan; heat and stir to dissolve gelatin. Mix fruit and gelatin together. Chill until nearly set. Fold in half of whipped cream. Pour into pie shell; chill until firm. Just before serving, garnish with remaining whipped cream and strawberries.

Grapefruit Meringue Pie

Preparation Time: 1 hour.

    1 9-inch baked pastry shell
    3 eggs, lightly beaten
    ¾ cup granulated sugar
    2 tablespoons cornstarch
    ⅓ cup grapefruit juice
    ½ cup butter
    2 tablespoons grated grapefruit rind
      Meringue

Preheat oven to 450°. Mix all filling ingredients except rind in saucepan. Cook over medium heat, whisking constantly, until mixture thickens and clears; add rind. Cool. Pour into pie shell. Prepare Meringue and spread onto filling, making sure to cover filling to edge of pie shell. Bake 6 to 8 minutes until lightly browned.

Meringue

    3 egg whites, room temperature
    ¼ teaspoon cream of tartar
    3 tablespoons granulated sugar

Beat egg whites in bowl until foamy. Add cream of tartar; gradually beat in sugar until shiny, stiff peaks form.

* * *

If you do not have fresh milk, substitute ½ cup evaporated milk and ½ cup water or ⅓ cup instant dry milk plus 1 cup water minus 1 tablespoon for every 1 cup of fresh milk.

Tart Crusts & Tarts

Paté Sucree (Sweet Tart Dough)

Makes 1 8- or 9-inch tart crust with lattice top.
Preparation Time: 30 minutes plus 30 minutes to chill.

 1½ cups flour
 1 tablespoon granulated sugar
 ½ cup butter
 1 egg yolk
 1 to 2 tablespoons ice water
 1 egg yolk, optional
 1 teaspoon water, optional

Mix flour and sugar in bowl; cut in butter with pastry blender until mixture is crumbly. Mix egg yolk with 1 tablespoon water; add to flour mixture. Mix with hands, adding as much of remaining 1 tablespoon water as needed to form smooth ball of dough. Wrap in waxed paper; chill 30 minutes. Roll out ⅔ of dough to 10-inch circle on lightly floured surface. Ease dough into 8- or 9-inch tart pan with removable bottom; gently press against bottom and up side of pan, trimming excess dough at rim. (*Do not* prick dough.) Roll remaining dough into 4 x 8-inch rectangle; cut lengthwise into ½-inch strips. Use strips to weave lattice pattern for top crust; see step 5C of Rolling and Fitting Pastry for Pies and Tarts. Brush lattice strips with 1 egg yolk beaten with 1 teaspoon water, if desired.

Note: For baked single crust, follow directions in step 1 of Baking Pie and Tart Crusts, using preheated 350° oven and baking 30 to 35 minutes. Cool before filling.

Food Processor Technique

 1 cup flour
 6 tablespoons frozen butter, cut into 6 pieces
 2 tablespoons granulated sugar
 1 egg yolk
 1 tablespoon cold water

Place flour, butter, sugar, egg yolk and water in work bowl of food processor fitted with metal blade. Process with on-off pulses 5 seconds. Continue processing with on-off pulses until dough forms ball. Wrap in waxed paper and chill 30 minutes. Dough may be rolled or pressed into 8- or 9-inch tart pan with removable bottom. Bake as directed above.

Butter Tart Crusts

Makes approximately 48 1¾-inch tart crusts.
Preparation Time: 45 minutes plus 30 minutes to chill.

 ½ cup butter *or* margarine
 ½ cup granulated sugar
 1 egg
 1 teaspoon vanilla
 2 cups flour

Mix butter, sugar, egg and vanilla at medium speed of electric mixer. Reduce speed to low; blend in flour. Shape dough into ball; wrap in waxed paper. Chill 30 minutes. Roll dough ⅛ inch thick on lightly floured surface. Cut 48 2¼-inch circles with cookie cutter. Press evenly into 1¾-inch muffin tins, trimming excess dough at rims. (Dough scraps can be rerolled to make additional tart crusts.)

Note: For baked tart crusts, follow directions in step 2 of Baking Pie and Tart Crusts. Cool before filling.

Cream Cheese Tart Crusts

Makes 36 1¾-inch tart crusts.
Preparation Time: 45 minutes plus 20 minutes to chill.

 ½ cup butter, softened
 1 3-ounce package cream cheese, softened
 2 tablespoons cream
 1¼ cups flour

Cream butter, cream cheese and cream in bowl; stir in flour. Divide into 3 balls. Wrap each in plastic wrap. Chill 30 minutes. Roll each ball into 6 x 8-inch rectangle ⅛ inch thick. Cut each rectangle into 12 2-inch squares. Press dough squares into 36 1¾-inch muffin tins, forming tart crusts. Trim excess dough at rims. Chill 20 minutes.

Note: For baked tart crusts, follow directions in step 2 of Baking Pie and Tart Crusts, baking 12 to 15 minutes. Cool before filling.

Glazed Fruit Tarts, page 36

Tart Crusts & Tarts

Tart Crusts

Makes 36 2¾-inch tart crusts.
Preparation Time: 45 minutes plus 1 to 2 hours to chill.

    2 cups flour
    1 tablespoon granulated sugar
    ½ cup butter, chilled
    3 tablespoons cold vegetable shortening
    5 to 6 tablespoons ice water

Combine flour and sugar in bowl; cut in butter and shortening with pastry blender until mixture resembles peas. Sprinkle water, 1 tablespoon at a time, on mixture. Toss lightly until ball of dough forms. Divide into 2 balls; flatten each and wrap each in plastic wrap. Chill 1 to 2 hours. Roll out 1 ball of dough to ⅛-inch thickness on lightly floured surface. Cut out 36 3-inch circles with cookie cutter. Press each into 2¾-inch muffin tins that are 1 inch deep; trim excess dough at rims. Dough scraps can be rerolled to make additional tart crusts, if desired.

Note: For baked tart crusts, follow directions in step 2 of Baking Pie and Tart Crusts. Freeze unbaked tart crusts 30 minutes. Bake 12 to 15 minutes. Cool before filling.

Glazed Fruit Tarts

Makes 24 1¾-inch tarts.
Preparation Time: 2 hours.

    24 baked 1¾-inch tart shells
    1 8-ounce package cream cheese, softened
    ½ cup granulated sugar
    2 tablespoons cream *or* milk
    2 tablespoons orange juice
    1 teaspoon grated orange rind
    1 pint strawberries, hulled *or* raspberries *or* blueberries
    Glaze

Beat cheese, sugar, cream, orange juice and orange rind in bowl until smooth. Fill shells ¾ full with mixture. Top with fruit of your choice; chill. Prepare Glaze; spoon over fruit. Chill.

Glaze

    1 tablespoon cornstarch
    ½ cup granulated sugar
    1 cup fresh *or* frozen strawberries, raspberries *or* blueberries, crushed (use same kind as selected above)
    1 teaspoon lemon juice

Mix cornstarch and sugar in saucepan; stir in crushed berries and lemon juice, cooking over medium heat until thick and clear; strain. Cool.

Variation

Green Grape Tart: Prepare as above, omitting Glaze. Instead reserve small amount of cream cheese mixture to pipe on top of each tart.

Macaroon Tarts

Makes 24 1¾-inch tarts.
Preparation Time: 1 hour, 30 minutes.

    1⅓ cups flour
    ¼ teaspoon salt
    ⅓ cup granulated sugar
    ½ cup butter *or* margarine, softened
    1 egg, beaten
    Filling
    Maraschino cherry slivers, to garnish

Preheat oven to 375°. Mix flour, salt and sugar in bowl; cut in butter with pastry blender until coarse crumbs form. Blend in egg. Knead dough slightly; wrap in plastic wrap or waxed paper. Chill 30 minutes. Place 1 tablespoon dough in 24 1¾-inch muffin cups. Press in bottoms and up sides of cups. Prepare Filling; spoon 1 tablespoon into each shell. Bake 18 to 20 minutes or until golden brown. Cool; remove from pans. Garnish with maraschino cherry slivers. Store in refrigerator.

Filling

    2 eggs, beaten
    1¼ cups granulated sugar
    1 cup flaked coconut
    1 teaspoon almond extract

Combine all ingredients in bowl.

Peach and Strawberry Tart

Makes 1 11-inch tart.
Preparation Time: 3 hours.

    ½ cup shortening
    1⅛ cups flour
    3 tablespoons water
    Filling
    1 16-ounce can sliced peaches, drained, reserve juice
    1 cup sliced strawberries
    Glaze

Preheat oven to 450°. Cut shortening into flour in bowl until crumbly. Sprinkle with water, 1 tablespoon at a time, mixing until dough gathers into ball. Wrap in plastic wrap; chill 1 hour. Roll dough into 12-inch circle on lightly floured board. Ease into 11-inch tart pan with removable bottom. Press onto bottom and side; trim at rim edge. Prick pastry on bottom and side of pan with tines of fork. Chill 30 minutes. Bake 8 to 10 minutes or until light brown. Cool on rack. Prepare Filling; spread over crust. Arrange peach slices in circle in middle of tart. Arrange strawberries along outer edge of tart. Prepare Glaze; spoon over fruit. Chill several hours.

Filling

    4 ounces cream cheese, softened
    2 teaspoons cream *or* milk
    2 teaspoons grated lemon peel
    1 teaspoon sugar
    ½ teaspoon vanilla

Beat all ingredients together in bowl.

Glaze

       Reserved peach juice
    1 tablespoon cornstarch
    2 tablespoons granulated sugar
    ⅛ teaspoon ground cinnamon
    1 teaspoon lemon juice

Add enough water to peach juice to measure 1 cup. Mix cornstarch, sugar and cinnamon in saucepan; stir in peach liquid. Heat to boiling, stirring constantly; boil 2 minutes. Remove from heat, stir in lemon juice and cool slightly.

Pecan Tarts

Makes 24 1¾-inch tarts.
Preparation Time: 2 hours, 20 minutes.

    ½ cup butter *or* margarine, softened
    1 3-ounce package cream cheese, softened
    1 cup flour
       Pecan Filling
    24 pecan halves

Preheat oven to 325°. Mix butter and cream cheese in bowl; cut mixture into flour until dough forms. Wrap in waxed paper; chill 1 hour. Divide into 24 1-inch balls; press onto bottoms and sides of 24 1¾-inch muffin cups. Chill. Prepare Pecan Filling; fill shells, topping each with pecan half. Bake 25 minutes. Cool on rack. Remove tarts from pans.

Pecan Filling

    1 egg
    ¾ cup light brown sugar, packed
    1 tablespoon butter, softened
    1 tablespoon light rum, optional
    1 teaspoon vanilla
    ⅛ teaspoon salt
    ½ cup chopped pecans

Blend all ingredients except pecans in bowl; stir in pecans.

Note: Prepared tarts may be frozen. Thaw before serving.

Butter Pecan Tarts

Makes 6 4-inch tarts.
Preparation Time: 1 hour, 10 minutes.

    6 4-inch baked tart shells
    ⅓ cup light brown sugar, packed
    1 tablespoon unflavored gelatin
       Dash salt
    3 eggs, separated
    ¾ cup milk
    1 teaspoon vanilla
    ¼ cup light brown sugar, packed
    1 cup chopped pecans
    2 tablespoons butter

Combine ⅓ cup brown sugar, gelatin and salt in saucepan; stir in beaten egg yolks and milk. Stir over low heat until thickened. Remove from heat; add vanilla. Chill until mixture mounds when dropped from spoon. Beat egg whites to soft peaks in bowl. Gradually beat in ¼ cup brown sugar until stiff peaks form. Fold gently into chilled gelatin mixture. Stir pecans in butter in skillet over medium heat, about 5 minutes. Mix ½ cup pecans into custard. Pour into tart shells; chill until firm. Garnish with remaining ½ cup pecans.

Pumpkin Tarts

Makes 24 1¾-inch tarts.
Preparation Time: 1 hour.

    24 baked 1¾-inch cream cheese tart crusts (see
       Pecan Tarts, Recipe on this page)
    ¼ cup light brown sugar, packed
    ⅛ teaspoon salt
    ⅛ teaspoon ground cinnamon
    ⅛ teaspoon ground nutmeg
    ⅛ teaspoon ground allspice
    ⅛ teaspoon ground cloves
    2 eggs, well beaten
    ¾ cup canned pumpkin
    ½ cup frozen whipped dessert topping, thawed *or* ½
       cup whipped cream
       Chopped nuts, optional

Combine all filling ingredients except whipped topping and nuts in saucepan. Stir over low heat 3 to 4 minutes until thickened. Remove from heat, cover and chill. Fold in topping; spoon about 3 teaspoons of mixture into each crust. Garnish with chopped nuts, if desired.

Note: Tarts may be frozen 2 to 3 months. Thaw in wrappings 30 to 45 minutes at room temperature.

Tart Crusts & Tarts

Fruit and Cheese Tarts

Makes 12 2¾-inch tarts.
Preparation Time: 3 hours.

- ½ cup butter *or* margarine, softened
- 1 5-ounce jar American cheese spread, room temperature
- 1½ cups flour
  Fruit Filling

Preheat oven to 375°. Combine butter and cheese spread in bowl. Cut into flour; blend to form dough. Shape into roll 1¼ inches in diameter; wrap in waxed paper. Chill 1 hour. Cut into 72 ⅛-inch slices. Place 1 slice in bottom of 12 2¾-inch muffin cups. Arrange 5 slices around side of each cup, overlapping slightly. Prick dough on bottom and side with tines of fork. Bake 18 to 20 minutes. Cool; carefully remove from pan. Fill with chilled Fruit Filling just before serving.

Fruit Filling

- ¼ cup granulated sugar
- 2 tablespoons cornstarch
- ⅛ teaspoon salt
- 1 8-ounce can crushed pineapple, drained, reserve juice
- 1 11-ounce can mandarin oranges, drained, reserve ½ cup juice
- 1 tablespoon lemon juice

Combine sugar, cornstarch, salt, pineapple, mandarin orange and lemon juices in saucepan. Cook, stirring, over medium heat until thickened. Stir in pineapple and mandarin oranges. Chill.

Fudgy Tarts

Makes 24 1¾-inch tarts.
Preparation Time: 2 hours, 10 minutes.

- 1 cup flour
- ¼ teaspoon baking powder
- ¼ teaspoon salt
- ½ cup shortening
- 1 egg, beaten
  Fudge Filling
- 24 small pecan halves

Preheat oven to 350°. Mix flour, baking powder and salt in bowl. Cut in shortening, using pastry blender, until mixture resembles tiny peas. Pour egg over mixture; stir to form dough. Chill 1 hour. Roll out on lightly floured board to less than ⅛-inch thickness. Cut into 24 2½-inch rounds; fit into 1¾-inch muffin cups. Chill 10 minutes. Prepare Fudge Filling. Place 1 scant tablespoon filling in each shell; top with pecan half. Bake 20

to 25 minutes. Cool; remove from pans. Store in refrigerator.

Fudge Filling

- 1 6-ounce package semisweet chocolate chips
- ½ cup granulated sugar
- 1 tablespoon milk
- 1 tablespoon butter
- 1 teaspoon instant coffee granules
- 1 teaspoon vanilla *or* rum flavoring
- 1 egg, beaten

Melt chocolate in saucepan; remove from heat. Stir in remaining ingredients.

Chocolate Fudge Tarts

Makes 48 1¾-inch tarts.
Preparation Time: 30 minutes.

- 48 unbaked 1¾-inch tart shells
- ½ cup butter
- 1½ ounces sweetened chocolate
- 2 eggs, beaten
- 1½ tablespoons light corn syrup
- ½ teaspoon vanilla
- ⅛ teaspoon salt
- ⅛ teaspoon ground cinnamon

Preheat oven to 350°. Melt butter and chocolate in saucepan. Cool. Add remaining filling ingredients. Fill shells; bake 20 minutes. Cool; remove from pans.

Cheese Tarts

Makes 24 1¾-inch tarts.
Preparation Time: 30 minutes.

- 24 unbaked 1¾-inch tart shells
- 1 8-ounce package cream cheese, softened
- ¼ cup granulated sugar
- 1 egg, beaten
- 1 tablespoon grated lemon rind
- 1 tablespoon lemon juice
- 1 teaspoon vanilla

Preheat oven to 350°. Combine all filling ingredients. Fill shells; bake 20 minutes. Cool; remove from pans. Store in refrigerator.

Fillings

Pastry Cream

Makes approximately 2 cups.
Preparation Time: 1 hour plus 2 hours to chill.

- 1½ cups milk *or* cream
- 4 egg yolks, room temperature
- ⅓ cup granulated sugar
- 3 tablespoons cornstarch
- 1 teaspoon vanilla
- 1 tablespoon orange-flavored liqueur, optional

Heat milk in saucepan. Beat yolks, sugar and cornstarch in bowl until mixture is light yellow and falls in a ribbon from beaters. Slowly pour hot milk into egg yolk mixture; return to saucepan. Heat, stirring constantly with wooden spoon, until thick, about 15 minutes. *Do not boil.* Strain into bowl; cool. Stir in vanilla and liqueur, if desired. Cover surface with plastic wrap. Chill 2 hours.

Note: Spread small amount of cream into baked tart crusts. Place 1 strawberry, 1 apricot half, 1 pineapple tidbit *or* 1 slice of kiwi fruit on top. Brush with Jelly Glaze (Recipe on page 41).

Quick Lemon Filling

Makes approximately 2¼ cups.
Preparation Time: 15 minutes.

- 1 3¾-ounce package instant lemon pie filling mix
- ⅛ teaspoon salt
- 1 tablespoon lemon juice
- 1 cup whipping cream, whipped

Prepare lemon filling mix according to package directions, adding salt and lemon juice. Fold in whipped cream.

Quick Pastry Cream

Makes approximately 2¼ cups.
Preparation Time: 20 minutes.

- 1 3¾-ounce package instant vanilla pudding mix
- 1 cup milk
- 1 cup whipping cream
- 1 tablespoon orange-flavored liqueur, optional

Prepare pudding mix as directed, substituting milk and whipping cream for liquid specified. Add liqueur, if desired.

Note: Fill baked pie *or* tart crusts with cream and top with blueberries, pitted cherries *or* raspberries. Decorate with dollops of whipped cream.

Chocolate Mousse

Makes approximately 6 cups.
Preparation Time: 20 minutes plus 2 hours to chill.

- 4 eggs, separated
- 1 12-ounce package semisweet chocolate chips
- 1 cup hot milk
- ½ teaspoon instant coffee granules *or* 1 tablespoon orange liqueur
- ½ cup granulated sugar

Blend egg yolks, chocolate chips, milk and coffee granules in blender until liquid. Beat egg whites in clean, dry bowl to soft peaks. Add sugar, 2 tablespoons at a time, beating until stiff peaks form. Fold into chocolate mixture. Chill 2 hours.

Creme Café

Makes approximately 3 cups.
Preparation Time: 30 minutes.

- ½ pound marshmallows
- 1 cup brewed coffee
- 2 tablespoons brandy
- 1 cup whipping cream, whipped and chilled

Melt marshmallows in coffee in top of double boiler over low heat. Cool. Add brandy; fold in whipped cream.

Note: Use to fill Cream Puffs (Recipe on page 43).

Mocha Cream

Makes approximately 2 cups.
Preparation Time: 15 minutes plus 2 hours to chill.

- 2 egg yolks, lightly beaten
- 1 cup milk
- 1 cup strong brewed coffee
- 1 3¾-ounce package instant chocolate pudding
- 2 tablespoons light brown sugar, packed
- ½ ounce unsweetened chocolate
- 2 tablespoons butter

Cook all ingredients except butter in saucepan, stirring, until mixture comes to a boil. Remove from heat; stir in butter. Cover surface with plastic wrap; chill 2 hours. Beat with spoon or whisk until smooth.

Glazes

Peach Glaze

Makes enough for 1 9-inch pie *or* 24 2¾-inch tarts *or* 48 1¾-inch tarts.
Preparation Time: 15 minutes.

  2 cups frozen sliced peaches, thawed and drained
  1 cup sour cream *or* sour half-and-half
  ½ cup confectioners' sugar
  1 teaspoon vanilla

Top cooked pie or tarts with peach slices. Mix sour cream with confectioners' sugar and vanilla. Spoon over peach slices. Chill.

Pineapple Glaze

Makes enough for 1 9-inch pie *or* 24 2¾-inch tarts *or* 48 1¾-inch tarts.
Preparation Time: 45 minutes.

  1 tablespoon cornstarch
  1 tablespoon granulated sugar
  1 20-ounce can crushed pineapple, drained, reserve juice
  ½ teaspoon vanilla
    Yellow food coloring, optional

Mix cornstarch and sugar in saucepan. Stir in pineapple juice; cook on low heat until thick and clear, about 5 minutes; remove from heat. Add vanilla, pineapple and 1 or 2 drops food coloring, if desired. Cool. Spread over filled pie or tarts. Chill until set.

Strawberry or Raspberry Glaze

Makes enough for 1 9-inch pie *or* 24 2¾-inch tarts *or* 48 1¾-inch tarts.
Preparation Time: 45 minutes.

  2½ tablespoons cornstarch
  1 cup granulated sugar
  1 cup water
  2 tablespoons lemon juice
    Red food coloring
  1 pint strawberries, washed and hulled *or* 1 pint raspberries, washed

Mix cornstarch and sugar in saucepan; add water gradually; stir until smooth. Cook over low heat, stirring constantly, until thick and clear, about 5 minutes. Add lemon juice and 1 or 2 drops food coloring. Cool. Glaze strawberries or raspberries on top of filled pie or tarts.

Blueberry Glaze

Makes enough for 1 9-inch pie *or* 24 2¾-inch tarts *or* 48 1¾-inch tarts.
Preparation Time: 45 minutes.

  2½ tablespoons cornstarch
  1 cup granulated sugar
  1 cup water
  1 pint blueberries, washed
  2 tablespoons lemon juice

Mix cornstarch and sugar in saucepan; add water gradually, stirring until smooth. Stir in ½ cup blueberries; stir constantly on low heat until thick and clear, about 5 minutes. Add lemon juice. Cool. Arrange remaining blueberries on top of filled pie or tarts; pour glaze over fruit. Chill until set.

Jelly Glaze

Makes enough for 1 9-inch pie *or* 24 2¾-inch tarts *or* 48 1¾-inch tarts.
Preparation Time: 10 minutes.

  1 cup red currant jelly *or* apple jelly

Melt in saucepan over low heat. Glaze fruit-filled pies or tarts.

Lemon Glaze

Makes enough for 1 9-inch pie *or* 24 2¾-inch tarts *or* 48 1¾-inch tarts.
Preparation Time: 45 minutes.

  ¾ cup granulated sugar
  2 tablespoons cornstarch
  ¼ teaspoon salt
  ½ cup water
  ½ cup lemon juice
  1 egg, lightly beaten
  1 tablespoon butter
  1 teaspoon grated lemon rind
  ½ teaspoon vanilla

Mix sugar, cornstarch and salt in saucepan; stir in water, lemon juice and egg. Cook over low heat, stirring constantly, until mixture comes to a boil, thickens and clears; remove from heat. Stir in butter, lemon rind and vanilla. Cool. Pour over cooled filled pie or tarts.

Note: Lemon Glaze is good on cheese pie.

Napoleons, Eclairs & Cream Puffs

Easy Napoleons

Makes 8.
Preparation Time: 2 hours, 30 minutes.

- 1 10-ounce package frozen patty shells, thawed in refrigerator overnight
- 1 3¾-ounce package instant French vanilla pudding mix
- 1 cup confectioners' sugar
- ½ teaspoon hot water
- ½ teaspoon vanilla
- 1 ounce unsweetened chocolate, melted

Preheat oven to 400°. Remove 2 patty shells from refrigerator at a time; press together on lightly floured board or cloth. Roll into 5 x 9-inch rectangle. Cut into 4 2¼ x 5-inch slices. Repeat with rest of patty shells. Place 1 inch apart on baking sheet; chill 30 minutes. Prick with tines of fork every ¼ inch. Bake 12 to 15 minutes until golden. Cool on rack. Prepare pudding mix using ½ cup less milk than directions specify; set aside. Stir together confectioners' sugar, water and vanilla in bowl to make thin glaze. Spread glaze on top of 8 rectangles. Before glaze dries, dip toothpick into chocolate and make thin lines ½ inch apart the length of rectangle. Draw toothpick across lines, alternating from side to side to give rippled effect. Spread filling on 16 rectangles; assemble Napoleons in 3 layers with glazed rectangle on top.

Easy Puff Pastry

Makes 8 to 10 napoleons.
Preparation Time: 1 hour, 15 minutes.

- 1 cup butter
- 1½ cups flour
- ½ cup dairy sour cream

Cut butter into flour in bowl until completely blended. Stir in sour cream to form dough. Chill 1 hour. Roll out into size desired for napoleons or pastries.

Napoleons

Makes 12.
Preparation Time: 45 minutes.

- Paté a Choux (Recipe on this page)
- Custard Filling
- Chocolate Icing

Prepare Custard Filling and Paté a Choux dough.

Preheat oven to 425°. Spread Paté a Choux on greased 10 x 15-inch jelly-roll pan. Prick with tines of fork at ¼-inch intervals. Bake 12 minutes. Cool. Cut into thirds, forming 3 5 x 10-inch pieces. Spread one rectangle with half of Custard Filling; top with second rectangle of dough and spread with remaining filling. Top with remaining rectangle. Prepare Chocolate Icing and spread over top. Chill until serving time.

Custard Filling

- 1 3¾-ounce instant French vanilla pudding mix
- 1¼ cups milk
- 1 cup whipping cream, whipped

Prepare pudding mix according to package directions using 1¼ cups milk, stirring until thickened. Chill. Fold in whipped cream.

Chocolate Icing

- ¼ cup butter or margarine
- 1½ ounces unsweetened chocolate
- ⅛ teaspoon salt
- 1½ cups confectioners' sugar
- 2 tablespoons milk
- 1 teaspoon vanilla

Melt butter and chocolate in saucepan over low heat. Add salt and confectioners' sugar; beat until smooth. Beat in milk and vanilla.

Paté a Choux

Makes 10 to 12 cream puffs or 30 to 40 small cream puffs or 8 swans or 16 eclairs.
Preparation Time: 1 hour.

- 1 cup water
- ½ cup butter or margarine
- 1 cup flour
- ¼ teaspoon salt
- 4 eggs

Bring water and butter to boil in saucepan. Add flour and salt all at once, beating with wooden spoon until mixture leaves side of pan and forms ball, 1 to 2 minutes; remove from heat. Add eggs, 1 at a time, beating thoroughly after each addition with hand-held electric mixer until dough is smooth; or place dough in work bowl of food processor fitted with steel blade. Add eggs 1 at a time and process until smooth.

Cream Puffs

Preheat oven to 400°. Drop dough from tablespoon or use pastry bag to form 2 x 1-inch circles

2½ inches apart on greased baking sheet. Bake 30 minutes or until golden. Reduce heat to 350°; bake 10 minutes. Remove from oven; pierce bottom or side of each puff with knife so steam can escape. Cool on rack. Split horizontally and fill with filling of your choice 1 hour before serving.

Small Cream Puffs

Preheat oven to 425°. Drop dough from teaspoon or use pastry bag to form 1 x ½-inch circles 2 inches apart on greased baking sheet. Bake 20 minutes. Pierce bottom or side of each puff; cool on rack. Split horizontally and fill with filling of your choice 1 hour before serving.

Swans

Preheat oven to 375°. Place dough in pastry bag fitted with ½-inch diameter tip. Pipe 8 3-inch long question-mark shapes on greased baking sheet to form swan heads and necks. Drop remaining batter into 8 round mounds 3 inches apart on greased baking sheet; smooth. Bake 20 minutes. Remove head portions; cool on rack. Bake puffs 45 minutes longer or until golden; cool on rack. About 1 hour before serving, cut top third off each puff; set aside. Spoon desired filling into bottom of puffs. Place swan necks into filling. Cut reserved tops in half; set into filling for wings. Chill until serving time.

Eclairs

Preheat oven to 375°. Pipe dough through pastry tube fitted with ¾-inch round tip or use 2 small spatulas to drop 16 rounded tablespoons of dough about 6 inches apart, in rows 2 inches apart, on greased baking sheet. Shape into 1 x 4-inch rectangles. Round sides and tops smoothly. Bake 45 minutes or until golden. Remove from oven, cut slit in side of each and return to oven 10 minutes. Cool on rack. About 1 hour before serving, split eclairs on 3 sides; spoon ice cream or desired filling into cavity of each. Glaze with Chocolate Glaze (Recipe on page 45).

Note: Cream puffs, swans and eclairs freeze well if unfilled. To thaw, place in preheated 425° oven 3 to 4 minutes or thaw on rack at room temperature 1 to 2 hours.

Spritz Puffs

Makes 12.
Preparation Time: 1 hour, 30 minutes.

   Paté a Choux (Recipe on page 43)
½ cup whipping cream
 2 tablespoons confectioners' sugar
½ teaspoon vanilla *or* orange-flavored liqueur
¾ cup apricot preserves *or* any desired flavor
   Confectioners' sugar, to garnish

Preheat oven to 400°. Place paté a choux dough in pastry bag fitted with star tip. Pipe 12 3-inch-long S shapes 2 inches apart on greased baking sheet. Bake 25 to 30 minutes. Cool on rack. Beat whipping cream, confectioners' sugar and vanilla in bowl until stiff peaks form. Cover and chill. About 1 hour before serving, cut each puff in half horizontally; scoop out any soft dough. Spoon 1 tablespoon preserves into bottom half of each puff; top with 1 rounded tablespoon of whipped cream. Replace top; chill until serving time. Sprinkle with confectioners' sugar.

Chocolate Nut Cream Puffs

Makes 10 to 12.
Preparation Time: 1 hour, 15 minutes.

½ cup butter *or* margarine
 1 cup boiling water
 1 cup flour
⅛ teaspoon salt
 3 tablespoons unsweetened cocoa
 1 tablespoon granulated sugar
 4 eggs
½ cup chopped pecans *or* walnuts

Preheat oven to 425°. Melt butter in boiling water in saucepan. Combine flour, salt, cocoa and sugar; add to boiling liquid all at once. Stir vigorously with wooden spoon until mixture leaves side of pan and forms ball; remove from heat. Cool slightly. Add eggs, 1 at a time, beating with hand-held electric mixer after each addition until dough is smooth. Stir in nuts. Shape into 10 to 12 round mounds on greased baking sheet. Bake 20 minutes. Reduce heat to 350°; bake 10 to 15 minutes. Remove puffs from oven; turn off oven. Split puffs in half horizontally; return to turned-off oven to dry 20 minutes. Remove excess dough from centers. Cool on racks.

Note: Fill with coffee ice cream *or* desired flavor. Top with fudge sauce.

Strawberry Cream Puffs

Makes 30 to 40.
Preparation Time: 30 minutes.

    30 to 40 Small Cream Puffs (Recipe on page 44)
    1 cup whipping cream
    ¼ cup confectioners' sugar
    1 tablespoon orange-flavored liqueur
    30 to 40 large strawberries, washed and hulled
        Confectioners' sugar, to garnish

Whip cream and confectioners' sugar to stiff peaks; stir in liqueur. Cover and chill. About 1 hour before serving, cut slice off puffs horizontally. Fill bottoms with 1 teaspoon whipped cream. Top with strawberry and dot of whipped cream. Cover with tops of cream puffs. Chill. Sprinkle with confectioners' sugar before serving.

Coffee Chantilly Filling

Makes approximately 2 cups.
Preparation Time: 10 minutes.

    1 cup whipping cream
    ½ cup confectioners' sugar
    2 teaspoons instant coffee granules
    1 teaspoon vanilla

Whip cream to soft peaks in chilled bowl. Add confectioners' sugar, coffee granules and vanilla; beat until stiff. Use to fill cream puffs *or* eclairs.

Pudding Filling

Makes approximately 2 cups.
Preparation Time: 10 minutes.

    Flavored instant pudding mix of your choice
    1½ cups milk
    ½ cup whipping cream, whipped *or* 1 cup dairy
        sour cream

Prepare pudding mix according to package directions using 1½ cups milk. Fold in whipped cream. Use to fill cream puffs *or* eclairs.

Whipped Cream Filling I

Makes approximately 2 cups.
Preparation Time: 1 hour, 10 minutes.

    1 cup whipping cream
    ½ cup confectioners' sugar
    1 teaspoon vanilla
    ¼ teaspoon almond extract

Combine cream, sugar and flavorings in chilled bowl; chill, with beaters, 1 hour. Beat until stiff. Use to fill cream puffs *or* eclairs.

Whipped Cream Filling II

Makes approximately 2 cups.
Preparation Time: 10 minutes.

    1 cup whipping cream
    1 tablespoon granulated sugar
    2 tablespoons brandy *or* orange-flavored liqueur,
        optional

Whip cream to soft peaks in small chilled bowl. Add sugar and brandy, if desired. Beat until stiff. Use to fill cream puffs *or* eclairs.

Fudge Sauce

Makes approximately 1 cup.
Preparation Time: 35 minutes.

    ⅓ cup white *or* brown creme de cacao *or* chocolate-
        mint liqueur
    2 ounces unsweetened chocolate
    2 tablespoons water
    2 tablespoons butter *or* margarine
    ⅛ teaspoon salt
    ½ cup granulated sugar
    2 tablespoons light corn syrup
    2 tablespoons brandy

Stir creme de cacao, chocolate, water, butter and salt in saucepan over low heat until smooth. Stir in sugar and corn syrup. Heat to boiling; simmer 5 minutes without stirring. Remove from heat; cool 10 minutes. Stir in brandy.

Note: Serve over ice cream-filled puffs *or* meringues. Sauce can be made ahead. Reheat in top of double boiler over medium heat.

Chocolate Glaze

Makes approximately 1 cup.
Preparation Time: 5 minutes.

    2 ounces semisweet chocolate, melted
    2 tablespoons butter *or* margarine, softened
    3 to 4 tablespoons milk
    1½ cups confectioners' sugar

Stir all ingredients together in bowl until smooth. Drizzle over cream puffs *or* eclairs.

Quick Chocolate Sauce

Makes approximately 1 cup.
Preparation Time: 5 minutes.

    1 6-ounce package semisweet chocolate chips
    ⅔ cup evaporated milk

Stir all ingredients in saucepan over low heat until chocolate is almost melted. Remove from heat; stir until smooth.

Apricot Bars

Makes 48 to 60.
Preparation Time: 1 hour, 30 minutes.

   1 pound dried apricots
   ½ cup granulated sugar
   1 teaspoon grated lemon rind
   2 tablespoons orange juice
   ½ cup water
   3 cups flour
   1 teaspoon baking powder
   3 cups quick-cooking rolled oats
1½ cups butter or margarine, softened
   2 cups light brown sugar, packed

Preheat oven to 350°. Cook apricots with ½ cup sugar, lemon rind, orange juice and water in saucepan over medium heat until apricots soften; cool. Mix flour, baking powder and oats in bowl. Cream butter and brown sugar in separate bowl. Stir dry ingredients into butter mixture until well blended. Press two-thirds of crumb mixture firmly onto bottom of 10 x 15-inch jelly-roll pan. Spread apricot mixture over crust. Sprinkle with remaining crumbs, patting gently. Bake 35 to 45 minutes or until brown. Cool slightly. Cut into squares. Store in airtight container.

Lemon Snow Bars

Makes 16.
Preparation Time: 45 minutes.

   1 cup flour
   ¼ cup granulated sugar
   ½ cup butter, softened
   2 eggs
   ¾ cup granulated sugar
   2 tablespoons flour
   ¼ teaspoon baking powder
   3 tablespoons lemon juice
   2 teaspoons grated lemon rind
     Confectioners' sugar

Preheat oven to 350°. Mix 1 cup flour and ¼ cup sugar in bowl; cut in butter until mixture resembles large peas. Pat into 8-inch square baking pan. Smooth with floured spatula. Bake 15 minutes or until edges are light brown. Beat eggs in bowl, gradually adding ¾ cup sugar, 2 tablespoons flour and baking powder. Stir in lemon juice and rind; beat well. Pour over crust. Bake 20 minutes. Sprinkle with confectioners' sugar. Cool. Cut into bars. Store in airtight container.

Chocolate Cheesecake Bars

Makes 24.
Preparation Time: 50 minutes.

   6 ounces chocolate wafer cookie crumbs
   3 tablespoons granulated sugar
   ½ teaspoon ground cinnamon
   3 tablespoons butter, melted
   2 8-ounce packages cream cheese, softened
   ½ cup granulated sugar
   1 egg
   ¼ teaspoon vanilla
   ¼ cup dairy sour cream
   ¼ cup coarsely chopped pecans, optional

Preheat oven to 350°. Mix crumbs, 3 tablespoons sugar, cinnamon and butter in bowl. Press firmly into greased 9 x 13-inch baking pan. Bake 5 minutes. Cool. Mix remaining ingredients except nuts in bowl; pour over crust. Sprinkle with nuts, if desired. Increase heat to 450°; bake 10 minutes. Reduce heat to 300°; bake 10 minutes. Cool. Cut into bars. Store in airtight container in refrigerator.

Pecan Caramel Triangles

Makes 72.
Preparation Time: 1 hour, 20 minutes.

1½ cups flour
   ⅛ teaspoon baking powder
   ½ cup granulated sugar
   6 tablespoons butter
   1 egg, lightly beaten
   1 tablespoon milk
   1 pound whole pecans
   2 cups butter
   1 pound light brown sugar
   ½ cup honey
   2 teaspoons vanilla

Preheat oven to 350°. Mix flour, baking powder and granulated sugar in bowl. Cut 6 tablespoons butter into flour mixture until it resembles peas. Mix in egg and milk; shape into dough. Pat into 10 x 15-inch jelly-roll pan. Bake 12 minutes. Remove from oven; place pecans on crust. Bring remaining ingredients to boil in saucepan, stirring constantly; boil 3 minutes. Pour over pecans. Bake 15 minutes. Cool 35 to 40 minutes. Cut into 72 triangles. Store in airtight container.

Bars

Chocolate Pecan Squares

Makes 24.
Preparation Time: 2 hours.

- 1 ounce unsweetened chocolate
- ¼ cup butter *or* margarine
- ½ cup granulated sugar
- 1 egg, beaten
- ¼ cup flour
- ¼ cup coarsely ground pecans *or* walnuts
- 1 cup confectioners' sugar
- 2 tablespoons butter *or* margarine, softened
- 1 tablespoon cream *or* nondairy creamer
- ½ teaspoon vanilla
- 3 ounces sweet chocolate
- 2 tablespoons semisweet chocolate chips
- 1 tablespoon butter *or* margarine

Preheat oven to 350°. Melt unsweetened chocolate and ¼ cup butter in saucepan; cool slightly. Blend in granulated sugar, egg, flour and nuts. Spread in greased 8-inch square baking pan. Bake 15 minutes. Cool. Beat confectioners' sugar, 2 tablespoons butter, cream and vanilla in bowl until smooth. Spread over chocolate layer. Chill 20 minutes. Melt remaining ingredients in saucepan over low heat; spread over filling. Chill 1 hour. Cut into squares. Store in airtight container.

Variation

Mint Filling: Beat together 1½ cups confectioners' sugar, ¼ cup melted butter and ⅓ cup green creme de menthe.

Chocolate Toffee Bars

Makes 48 to 72.
Preparation Time: 45 minutes.

- 1 cup margarine *or* butter, softened
- 1 cup light brown sugar, packed
- 1 teaspoon vanilla
- 1 egg
- 2 cups flour
- 2 4-ounce squares sweet chocolate, broken into pieces
- ¾ cup finely chopped nuts

Preheat oven to 350°. Cream margarine and sugar in bowl until fluffy. Beat in vanilla and egg. Add flour gradually, beating constantly. Spread evenly in 10 x 15-inch jelly-roll pan. Bake 20 to 25 minutes. While hot, top with chocolate pieces, spreading evenly. Sprinkle with nuts. Cool. Cut into bars. Store in airtight container.

Butter Pecan Bars

Makes 48.
Preparation Time: 1 hour plus 1 hour to chill.

- 1 cup butter *or* margarine
- 1 cup light brown sugar, packed
- 1 egg yolk
- 1 teaspoon vanilla
- 2 cups flour
- 1 6-ounce package butterscotch chips
- 2 tablespoons butter
- ⅓ cup light corn syrup
- 1 tablespoon water
- 1 cup pecan halves

Preheat oven to 350°. Cream 1 cup butter and brown sugar in bowl. Mix in egg yolk, vanilla and flour. Spread in 9 x 13-inch baking pan. Bake 25 minutes. Cool. Melt butterscotch chips and 2 tablespoons butter in saucepan over low heat. Add corn syrup and water; stir until smooth; cool. Spread butterscotch mixture over crust. Sprinkle with nuts, pressing them in lightly. Chill 1 hour. Cut into squares. Store in airtight container in refrigerator or freezer.

Note: Thaw in container at room temperature.

Butterscotch-Chocolate Chip Bars

Makes 36.
Preparation Time: 50 minutes.

- 1 cup flour
- 1 cup quick-cooking rolled oats
- ¾ cup light brown sugar, packed
- ¼ teaspoon baking soda
- ¾ cup butter *or* margarine, melted
- 1 teaspoon vanilla
- 1 6-ounce package semisweet chocolate chips
- ½ cup chopped nuts, optional
- ¾ cup butterscotch topping
- 3 tablespoons flour

Preheat oven to 350°. Mix 1 cup flour, oats, brown sugar, baking soda, butter and vanilla in bowl. Press one-half of mixture into 9-inch square baking pan. Bake 15 minutes. Sprinkle chocolate chips and nuts over hot crust. Mix topping with 3 tablespoons flour; pour over chips and nuts. Sprinkle remaining crumb mixture on top. Bake 20 minutes. Cool; cut into bars. Store in airtight container.

Fudgie Nut Bars

Makes 75.
Preparation Time: 1 hour.

  1 cup butter *or* **margarine, softened**
  2 cups light brown sugar, packed
  2 eggs
  2 teaspoons vanilla
2½ cups flour
  1 teaspoon baking soda
  3 cups quick-cooking rolled oats
  1 12-ounce package semisweet chocolate chips
  2 tablespoons butter *or* **margarine**
  1 14-ounce can sweetened condensed milk
  ¼ teaspoon salt
  1 cup chopped nuts
  2 teaspoons vanilla

Preheat oven to 350°. Cream 1 cup butter and brown sugar in bowl until fluffy; beat in eggs and 2 teaspoons vanilla. Combine flour, baking soda and oats. Stir into creamed mixture; reserve 1½ cups for topping. Press remaining mixture into 10 x 15-inch jelly-roll pan. Stir chocolate chips, 2 tablespoons butter, milk and salt in saucepan over low heat until melted. Remove from heat; stir in nuts and 2 teaspoons vanilla. Spread over crust. Sprinkle with reserved crumb mixture. Bake 25 minutes or until lightly browned. Cool. Cut into bars. Store in airtight container.

Apricot Coconut Bars

Makes 24 to 36.
Preparation Time: 1 hour, 10 minutes.

  1 cup flour
  ¼ cup granulated sugar
  ½ cup margarine *or* **butter**
  ½ cup cold water
1¼ cups nonfat dry milk powder
  ¾ cup granulated sugar
  ⅓ cup flour
  ½ teaspoon baking powder
  2 eggs, beaten
3½ ounces flaked coconut
  6 ounces dried apricots, cut into small pieces

Preheat oven to 350°. Mix 1 cup flour and ¼ cup sugar in bowl. Cut in margarine with pastry blender until mixture is crumbly. Press firmly onto bottom of 9-inch square baking pan. Bake 25 minutes. Cool on rack. Mix water and milk powder in small saucepan until smooth. Gradually stir in ¾ cup sugar over medium heat until sugar dissolves; cool. Mix remaining ingredients and add to milk. Spread over crust. Bake 35 minutes or until firm to touch. Cool in pan; cut into squares. Store in airtight container.

Honey-Date Fingers

Makes 36 to 48.
Preparation Time: 30 minutes.

  1 cup honey
  3 eggs, beaten
  1 teaspoon vanilla
1⅓ cups flour
  1 teaspoon baking powder
  1 cup chopped almonds
  1 pound dates, chopped
  Confectioners' sugar

Preheat oven to 350°. Mix honey, eggs and vanilla in bowl. Combine flour, baking powder, nuts and dates; stir into egg mixture. Pour into greased 9 x 13-inch baking pan. Bake 15 to 20 minutes. Cool. Cut into thin strips or squares. Sprinkle with confectioners' sugar. Store in airtight container.

Chocolate Cream Squares

Makes 16.
Preparation Time: 1 hour, 10 minutes.

  8 ounces semisweet chocolate
  6 eggs, separated
  ½ teaspoon vanilla
  ⅓ cup granulated sugar
  ⅓ cup flour
1½ cups whipping cream
  ⅓ cup unsweetened cocoa
  ⅓ cup granulated sugar
  2 tablespoons water

Preheat oven to 350°. Grate 4 ounces of the chocolate; set aside. Beat egg whites in clean bowl until stiff peaks form; set aside. Beat egg yolks, vanilla and ⅓ cup sugar in separate bowl with same beaters until thick. Beat in flour and grated chocolate; fold in whites. Pour into 2 greased 8-inch square baking pans. Bake 15 minutes or until toothpick inserted in center comes out clean. Cool in pans on racks 15 minutes. Loosen edges of cakes with spatula; turn onto racks. Cool completely. Beat cream, cocoa and ⅓ cup sugar until stiff. Spread over 1 cake; chill 2 hours. Melt remaining 4 ounces chocolate in saucepan with water, stirring constantly. Spread over remaining cake layer; allow to set. Place chocolate-covered cake on top of cream-covered cake. Cut into squares. Store in airtight container in refrigerator.

Butterhorns

Butterhorns

Makes 24.
Preparation Time: 1 hour, 10 minutes plus 8 hours to chill.

    1 cup butter, softened
    1 package active dry yeast
    ¼ cup granulated sugar
    3 egg yolks, beaten
    1 cup evaporated milk
    3 cups flour
    2 egg whites
    ¼ cup granulated sugar
    1 teaspoon ground cinnamon
    ½ cup chopped nuts, raisins, currants, coconut or
      Almond Paste Filling
      Icing or confectioners' sugar

Preheat oven to 350°. Pour butter over yeast and ¼ cup sugar in bowl; beat, adding egg yolks and milk. Blend in flour to form smooth dough. Place in greased bowl; cover and chill overnight. Divide dough into thirds; return all but 1 portion to refrigerator. Roll out each third on a lightly floured board into a circle; cut into 8 triangles. Beat egg whites in bowl until foamy; add ¼ cup sugar and cinnamon, beating until stiff peaks form. Spread to ½-inch of edge of triangles; top with nuts or desired filling. Roll from wide end; bend into crescent shape. Place, pointed-seam-side down, on baking sheet. Bake 15 to 20 minutes. Frost with Icing or sprinkle with confectioners' sugar.

Almond Paste Filling

Makes approximately 1 cup.
Preparation Time: 5 minutes.

    ¼ pound almonds, blanched
    ½ cup granulated sugar
    1 egg, lightly beaten

Grind nuts and sugar in blender or food processor. Add egg; work until smooth.

Icing

    1 cup confectioners' sugar
    1 tablespoon butter or margarine
    1 teaspoon vanilla or almond extract
      Hot milk (about 2 tablespoons)

Mix confectioners' sugar, butter and vanilla in bowl. Gradually add enough milk for spreading consistency.

Hungarian Butterhorns

Makes 128 miniatures.
Preparation Time: 1 hour plus 3 hours to chill.

    4 cups flour
    ¼ teaspoon salt
    1 package active dry yeast
    1¼ cups shortening
    3 egg yolks
    ⅔ cup dairy sour cream
    1 teaspoon vanilla
      Filling
      Confectioners' sugar or Glaze

Preheat oven to 375°. Mix flour, salt and yeast in bowl. Cut in shortening with pastry blender. Mix yolks, sour cream and vanilla in bowl. Add to dry ingredients and blend to form dough. Divide into 16 parts; form each into flattened ball. Wrap each in plastic wrap; chill 3 hours. Roll out each ball of dough to 9-inch circle on board sprinkled with confectioners' sugar. Cut each circle into 8 wedges; spread each wedge with 2 teaspoons Filling. Starting from wide end roll toward tip; shape into crescent and place, pointed-seam-side down, on baking sheet. Repeat with remaining dough. Bake 12 minutes. Sprinkle with confectioners' sugar or drizzle with Glaze.

Filling

    3 egg whites, room temperature
    ¾ cup granulated sugar
    1 teaspoon vanilla
    1 cup finely chopped nuts or ½ cup chopped nuts
      mixed with ½ cup semisweet chocolate chips

Beat egg whites in bowl until stiff peaks form. Gradually add sugar, continuing to beat. Fold in vanilla and nuts.

Glaze

    1½ cups confectioners' sugar
    2 tablespoons boiling water
    1 teaspoon lemon juice

Combine ingredients in bowl; beat until smooth.

Butterhorns

Filled Crescents I

Makes 36.

Preparation Time: 1 hour, 10 minutes plus 3 hours to chill.

- **1 cup butter** or **margarine, softened**
- **2 cups flour**
- **1 cup dairy sour cream**
- **1 egg, lightly beaten**
- **½ cup apricot preserves** or **filling of your choice**
- **½ cup finely chopped walnuts**
  Confectioners' sugar

Preheat oven to 375°. Cut butter into flour in bowl with pastry blender until coarse crumbs form. Stir in sour cream and egg to form dough. Divide dough into thirds; form each third into a ball and wrap in plastic wrap. Chill 3 hours or overnight. Roll out one-third at a time on lightly floured board to 10- to 11-inch circle. Spread with ⅓ of preserves; sprinkle with ⅓ of nuts. Cut dough into 12 triangles with sharp knife. Roll each triangle starting at wide end to opposite point; form into crescent. Place, pointed-seam-side down, on baking sheet. Repeat with remaining dough, preserves and nuts. Bake 20 minutes or until golden. Cool on rack. Sprinkle with confectioners' sugar.

Filled Crescents II

Makes 36.

Preparation Time: 1 hour plus 8 hours to chill.

- **¾ cup cold butter**
- **¼ cup cream cheese**
- **2 cups flour**
- **1 egg, separated**
- **¾ cup dairy sour cream**
- **⅔ cup heavy filling (apricot preserves, cherry preserves, poppy seed filling)** or **marzipan**
  Confectioners' sugar

Preheat oven to 350°. Cut butter and cream cheese into flour in bowl with pastry blender until crumbly. Lightly beat egg yolk and combine with sour cream in separate bowl; add to flour mixture. Stir vigorously until dough leaves side of bowl. Place on lightly floured cloth; knead 1 minute. Divide dough into thirds, forming each into flat circle; wrap each in waxed paper. Chill 8 hours or up to several days. Roll each third into 12-inch circle; cut into 12 equal wedges. Place 1 teaspoon filling on wide end of each wedge. Starting at wide end, roll to tip. Brush tip with beaten egg white; form into crescent shape;

place on baking sheet, pointed-seam-side down. Bake 20 to 25 minutes or until golden. Cool and dust with confectioners' sugar.

Miniature Pecan Rolls

Makes 48.

Preparation Time: 1 hour, 30 minutes plus 8 hours to chill.

- **3 cups flour**
- **½ cup granulated sugar**
- **1 teaspoon salt**
- **1 envelope active dry yeast**
- **½ cup cream** or **milk**
- **¾ cup butter**
- **½ cup dairy sour cream**
- **2 eggs, lightly beaten**
- **¼ cup butter, melted**
- **½ cup granulated sugar mixed with 1 teaspoon ground cinnamon**
- **½ cup chopped nuts**
- **½ cup currants**
- **96 pecan halves**
  Syrup

Mix flour, ½ cup sugar, salt and yeast in bowl. Heat cream in saucepan and stir in ¾ cup butter until melted. Stir sour cream into eggs in bowl. Beat cream-butter and sour cream-egg mixtures into flour. Cover and chill overnight. Preheat oven to 350°. Divide dough into 4 parts. Roll each part into 3 x 12-inch rectangle on lightly floured board. Brush dough rectangle with 1 tablespoon melted butter; sprinkle with 2 tablespoons sugar-cinnamon mixture. Spread with 2 tablespoons chopped nuts and 2 tablespoons currants. Roll from long side and cut into 12 slices. Repeat with remaining dough and filling. Place 2 pecan halves in bottom of each of 48 1¾-inch muffin tins. Pour ½ teaspoon Syrup over pecans and top with slice of dough. Bake 15 to 20 minutes. Cool slightly and remove from tins.

Syrup

- **2 tablespoons light corn syrup**
- **1 cup light brown sugar, packed**
- **¼ cup butter**
- **1 tablespoon water**

Bring all ingredients to boil in saucepan and stir well.

Brownies

Chocolate-Caramel Brownies

Makes 48.
Preparation Time: 1 hour plus 1 hour to chill.

- ¾ cup caramel ice cream topping
- 3 tablespoons flour
- 1 8½-ounce package German chocolate cake mix
- ½ cup butter *or* margarine, melted
- ⅓ cup evaporated milk
- 1 teaspoon vanilla
- ½ cup chopped pecans *or* walnuts
- 1 6-ounce package semisweet chocolate chips

Preheat oven to 350°. Mix caramel topping and flour in bowl; set aside. Stir cake mix, butter, milk, vanilla and nuts in bowl to form dough. Press half of dough into greased and floured 9 x 13-inch baking pan. Bake 8 minutes. Sprinkle with chocolate chips; spread caramel mixture over the chips. Drop spoonfuls of remaining dough over caramel mixture. Bake 15 to 18 minutes. Cool on rack. Chill 1 hour. Cut into 48 bars. Store in airtight container.

Chocolate Chip Brownies

Makes 16.
Preparation Time: 50 minutes.

- ¾ cup flour
- ¼ teaspoon baking soda
- ⅛ teaspoon salt
- ⅓ cup margarine *or* butter
- ¾ cup granulated sugar
- 2 tablespoons water
- 1 12-ounce package semisweet chocolate chips
- ½ teaspoon vanilla
- 2 eggs
- ½ cup chopped nuts

Preheat oven to 325°. Mix flour, baking soda and salt in bowl; set aside. Bring margarine, sugar and water to a boil in saucepan; remove from heat. Stir in half of chocolate chips until melted; stir in vanilla. Place in large bowl; beat in eggs. Stir in flour mixture and remaining chocolate chips and nuts. Spread into greased 9-inch square baking pan. Bake 30 to 35 minutes. Cool. Cut into 16 squares. Store in airtight container.

Note: Recipe may be doubled and baked in 9 x 13-inch pan.

Fudge Brownies

Makes 36.
Preparation Time: 45 minutes.

- ½ cup butter *or* margarine, softened
- 1 cup granulated sugar
- 1 teaspoon vanilla
- 2 eggs
- 2 ounces unsweetened chocolate, melted
- ½ cup flour
- ½ cup chopped walnuts, optional

Preheat oven to 325°. Cream butter, sugar and vanilla in bowl; beat in eggs. Blend in chocolate, flour and nuts, if desired. Spread in greased 7 x 11-inch *or* 8-inch square baking pan. Bake 20 to 25 minutes. Cool. Cut into squares. Store in airtight container.

Julie's Brownies

Makes 36.
Preparation Time: 1 hour.

- ½ cup butter *or* margarine, softened
- 4 ounces unsweetened chocolate, melted
- 2 cups granulated sugar
- 2 eggs
- 1 teaspoon vanilla
- 1 cup flour
- 1 cup coarsely chopped nuts

Preheat oven to 325°. Cream butter, chocolate and sugar in bowl; beat in eggs and vanilla. Stir in flour and nuts. Spread in greased 7 x 11-inch baking pan. Bake 35 to 40 minutes. Cool. Cut into squares. Stir in airtight container.

Variations

Coconut: Substitute ¾ cup flaked coconut for nuts.

Mocha: Add 4 teaspoons instant coffee granules with the sugar.

Date and Nut: Add ½ cup chopped dates and nuts.

Brown Sugar: Substitute 1 cup light brown sugar, packed, for granulated sugar.

Filled Brownies: Split each brownie in half; put together filled with frosting of your choice.

Petits Fours

Easy Petits Fours

Makes 60.
Preparation Time: 4 hours, 30 minutes.

    2 17-ounce packages pound cake mix
    4 eggs
      Apricot Glaze
      Frosting

Preheat oven to 350°. Prepare pound cake mixes as directed, using 4 eggs and liquid specified. Spread in lightly greased and floured 10 x 15-inch jelly-roll pan. Bake 30 to 35 minutes or until cake springs back when pressed. Cool. Cut 60 1¼-inch shapes with knife. Place cakes, one at a time, on fork; spoon prepared Apricot Glaze over, covering top and sides of cake. Place on racks until glaze sets, about 1 hour. Prepare Frosting. Place glazed cake on fork; spoon Frosting over cake so it runs over top and down sides. Let dry on racks 1 hour. Frost again if cakes are not completely covered; let dry. Decorate tops with frosting flowers and leaves or drizzles of Frosting. Chill several hours on waxed paper-covered trays. Store in airtight container in refrigerator.

Apricot Glaze

    1½ cups apricot preserves
    ½ cup granulated sugar
    ½ cup water
    1 tablespoon lemon juice

Bring all ingredients except lemon juice to boil in saucepan; boil, stirring, 5 minutes. Add lemon juice; strain and cool.

Frosting

    2¾ cups granulated sugar
    ⅛ teaspoon salt
    ¼ teaspoon cream of tartar
    1½ cups water
    3 cups sifted confectioners' sugar
    ½ teaspoon almond extract
      Yellow food coloring

Cook sugar, salt, cream of tartar and water in saucepan over low heat, stirring until sugar dissolves. Increase heat to medium and cook, without stirring, to 226° on a candy thermometer. Pour mixture into top of double boiler; cool to 110°. Beat in just enough confectioners' sugar to make frosting thick enough to coat wooden spoon, but thin enough to pour. Add extract and food coloring; mix. Keep frosting over hot water. If it is too thin, stir in more confectioners' sugar. If it is too thick, thin with a little warm water.

Petits Fours

Makes approximately 117.
Preparation Time: 50 minutes.

    6 tablespoons butter, softened
    1 cup granulated sugar
    2 eggs
    1½ cups flour
    1½ teaspoons baking powder
    ¼ teaspoon salt
    ½ cup milk
    1 teaspoon vanilla
      Grated rind of 1 lemon
    ⅔ cup granulated sugar
      Juice of 1 lemon

Preheat oven to 350°. Cream butter and 1 cup sugar in bowl; beat in eggs, flour, baking powder, salt, milk, vanilla and lemon rind. Pour into greased 9 x 13-inch baking pan. Bake 25 minutes. Mix ⅔ cup sugar with lemon juice in bowl; immediately spoon mixture over top of cake; bake 5 minutes. Cut warm cake into 1-inch squares. Store, covered, in refrigerator.

Note: Petits fours freeze well if tightly wrapped.

Genoise

Light yellow cake for Petits Fours.
Makes 1 8-inch cake.
Preparation Time: 1 hour plus 1 hour cooling time.

    3 large eggs
    ½ cup granulated sugar
    2 teaspoons vanilla
      Grated rind of 1 lemon
    ⅛ teaspoon salt
    ⅔ cup cake flour
    ¼ cup butter, melted

Preheat oven to 350°. Beat eggs, sugar, vanilla, lemon rind and salt in bowl with electric mixer 10 minutes or more until ribbon of batter falls from beaters when they are lifted. Sift and fold one-fourth of the flour into batter, then another one-fourth of the flour and one-half of melted butter. Continue alternately to fold in remaining

flour and butter. (Do not stir in any milky residue of melted butter.) *Do not overmix.* Line 8-inch square baking pan with waxed paper; butter and lightly flour the paper. Spoon batter into prepared pan. Bake 25 to 30 minutes or until cake pulls away from edges of pan. Cool on rack 10 minutes. Invert cake onto rack; peel off paper. Cool at least 2 hours before frosting.

Note: Genoise can be frozen if tightly wrapped.

Chocolate Fudge Cakes

These are better than brownies because they taste like fudge and look like petits fours.

Makes 72 to 84.
Preparation Time: 1 hour.

    1 cup water
    1 cup butter *or* margarine
    ¼ cup unsweetened cocoa
    2 cups flour
    2 cups granulated sugar
    1 teaspoon baking soda
    ½ teaspoon salt
    ½ teaspoon ground cinnamon
    1 cup dairy sour cream *or* ½ cup buttermilk
    2 eggs
    1 teaspoon vanilla
      Chopped nuts, optional

Preheat oven to 350°. Bring water, butter and cocoa to boil in saucepan; remove from heat. Combine flour, sugar, baking soda, salt and cinnamon in bowl. Add hot cocoa mixture; beat until smooth. Beat in sour cream, eggs and vanilla. Pour into greased 10 x 15-inch jelly-roll pan. Bake 20 to 30 minutes. Prepare Frosting. Pour over hot cake. Cool and cut into squares or diamonds. Sprinkle tops with chopped nuts, if desired.

Frosting

    ½ cup butter
    ¼ cup unsweetened cocoa
    6 tablespoons milk *or* buttermilk
    1 teaspoon instant coffee granules
    ⅛ teaspoon ground cinnamon
    1 pound confectioners' sugar
    1 teaspoon vanilla

Bring butter, cocoa, milk and coffee granules to boil in saucepan; remove from heat. Beat in cinnamon, confectioners' sugar and vanilla until smooth.

Note: These freeze well.

Carrot-Pineapple Mini Cakes

Makes 60 to 72.
Preparation Time: 1 hour.

    2 eggs
    ¾ cup vegetable oil
    1 teaspoon vanilla
    1 8-ounce can crushed pineapple, drained, reserve juice
  1½ cups flour
    1 cup granulated sugar
    1 teaspoon baking soda
    ½ teaspoon baking powder
    ½ teaspoon ground cinnamon
    ½ teaspoon salt
    1 cup grated carrots
    ½ cup chopped walnuts
    ½ cup currants, optional
      Cream Cheese Frosting

Preheat oven to 350°. Beat eggs, oil, vanilla and pineapple juice in large bowl. Add flour, sugar, baking soda, baking powder, cinnamon and salt. Stir in pineapple, carrots, nuts and currants, if desired. Grease and flour 1¾-inch cupcake pans. Place 1 tablespoon batter in each cup. Bake 15 minutes or until toothpick inserted in center comes out clean. Remove from pans; cool on rack. Place in paper cups; frost tops with Cream Cheese Frosting. Store in airtight container in refrigerator.

Cream Cheese Frosting

    2 tablespoons butter *or* margarine, softened
    1 3-ounce package cream cheese, softened
    1 tablespoon vanilla
    1 tablespoon orange juice
    2 cups confectioners' sugar

Cream butter and cream cheese in bowl until fluffy; beat in vanilla and orange juice. Add sugar gradually, beating until smooth and creamy.

Small Sweets

Date-Nut Roll

Makes 48 slices.
Preparation Time: 1 hour.

- **4 eggs, lightly beaten**
- **2 cups granulated sugar**
- **¼ cup margarine** *or* **butter**
- **1 cup chopped dates**
- **2 teaspoons vanilla**
- **4 cups crisp rice cereal**
- **1 cup chopped walnuts**
  Flaked coconut

Mix eggs and sugar in saucepan. Stir in margarine over medium heat. Add dates, stirring constantly. When mixture forms ball, add vanilla. Pour hot mixture over cereal and walnuts in bowl; mix well. Divide into 4 8-inch long rolls. Roll each in coconut; wrap in foil. Chill. Cut each roll into 12 slices.

Honey-Almond Sticks with Chocolate Glaze

Makes 26 to 30.
Preparation Time: 1 hour, 10 minutes.

- **½ cup butter, softened**
- **2 tablespoons honey**
- **½ teaspoon almond extract**
- **1 cup flour**
- **¾ cup finely chopped almonds**
  Chocolate Glaze

Preheat oven to 350°. Cream butter in bowl; add honey and almond extract. Gradually stir in flour until well blended; stir in nuts. Cover and chill 30 minutes. Shape dough by tablespoonfuls into 2½ x 3-inch sticks. Place 1 inch apart on ungreased baking sheets. Bake 12 to 15 minutes or until golden. Cool on rack. Prepare Chocolate Glaze; spread on ½ of each stick. Return to rack to set.

Chocolate Glaze

- **1½ ounces semisweet chocolate**
- **1 tablespoon butter** *or* **margarine**
- **2 teaspoons light corn syrup**

Melt chocolate in small saucepan over low heat; add butter and corn syrup. Blend.

Party Cookies

Makes 36 to 48.
Preparation Time: 40 minutes.

- **1 cup butter, softened**
- **¼ cup confectioners' sugar**
- **2 cups flour**
- **1 teaspoon vanilla**
  Chocolate Glaze
- **½ cup finely chopped nuts** *or* **chocolate jimmies**
  Confectioners' sugar, optional

Preheat oven to 400°. Blend butter, ¼ confectioners' sugar, flour and vanilla together to form dough. Shape into 1½-inch almond shapes, logs or balls. Place on baking sheet. Bake 10 minutes. Cool on rack; dip one half of each cookie into Chocolate Glaze and then into nuts or chocolate jimmies *or* if desired, roll baked cookies in confectioners' sugar while still warm. Store in airtight container.

Chocolate Glaze

- **½ cup semisweet chocolate chips**

Melt in saucepan over low heat; stir until smooth.

Retha's Mini Fruitcakes

Makes 48.
Preparation Time: 1 hour, 10 minutes.

- **¾ cup flour**
- **½ teaspoon baking powder**
- **½ teaspoon salt**
- **2 cups cranberries, washed and dried**
- **1 8-ounce package pitted dates, cut up**
- **2½ cups coarsely chopped pecans**
- **2 eggs**
- **¾ cup granulated sugar**
- **1 teaspoon lemon juice** *or* **vanilla**

Preheat oven to 300°. Mix flour, baking powder and salt in bowl. Stir in cranberries, dates and nuts; toss well. Beat eggs in bowl, adding sugar and lemon juice. Pour over dry mixture; mix. Spoon into 48 paper-lined 1¾-inch muffin cups. Bake 45 to 50 minutes. Remove from paper liners while still warm. Cool. Store in airtight container.

Pirouettes

Makes 30 to 36.
Preparation Time: 1 hour, 15 minutes.

½ cup butter, softened
½ cup granulated sugar
1 teaspoon vanilla
2 egg whites
⅔ cup flour
Chocolate Filling

Preheat oven to 375°. Cream butter, sugar and vanilla in bowl until fluffy; beat in egg whites. Stir in flour just until blended. Drop by teaspoonfuls 1-inch apart on baking sheet. Spread with spatula to 3-inch circles. Bake on middle oven rack 5 minutes or until edges are light brown. Loosen, 1 cookie at a time, from baking sheet with spatula. Working quickly, turn over and roll tightly around a pencil. Cool seam-side-down on rack. Fill pirouettes with Chocolate Filling using pastry bag, or frost insides with wooden pick or soda straw.

Chocolate Filling

3 ounces semisweet chocolate chips
¼ teaspoon vegetable oil, butter or margarine

Melt chocolate with oil in saucepan over low heat; stir until smooth.

Viennese Fingers

Makes 24.
Preparation Time: 1 hour, 45 minutes.

1 cup flour
½ cup butter or margarine, softened
½ cup finely chopped walnuts or pecans
¼ cup confectioners' sugar
½ teaspoon vanilla
¼ teaspoon almond extract
Chocolate Glaze
Chocolate jimmies, nonpareils or flaked coconut

Mix first 6 ingredients in bowl; shape into flat ball. Wrap in waxed paper. Chill 45 minutes. Divide into 24 balls; roll each into 3-inch length, curving into crescent shape, or roll each into 2-inch length, shaping into oval. Place on baking sheet. Preheat oven to 375°. Bake 10 minutes or until set but not brown. Let set 1 minute. Cool on rack. Prepare Chocolate Glaze; dip ends in glaze, then into jimmies, nonpareils or flaked coconut. Chill until serving time.

Chocolate Glaze

1½ ounces semisweet chocolate
1½ teaspoons light corn syrup
1½ teaspoons cream

Melt chocolate with corn syrup and cream in saucepan over low heat; stir to mix.

Baklava

Make this divine Greek pastry a day ahead.

Makes approximately 54 pieces.
Preparation Time: 1 hour, 30 minutes.

21 sheets phyllo dough, thawed in wrappings
7 cups chopped walnuts
1 tablespoon ground cinnamon
½ cup granulated sugar
1½ cups butter or combination butter and margarine, melted
Syrup

Cut phyllo sheets in half crosswise to fit in bottom of greased 9 x 13-inch baking pan. Cover sheets with damp towel. Mix nuts, cinnamon and sugar in bowl. Layer 9 half sheets of phyllo in pan, brushing each with melted butter. Sprinkle 1 cup nut mixture over phyllo sheets in pan; drizzle with some butter. Top with 4 half sheets, brushing each with melted butter. Sprinkle with 1 cup nuts and drizzle with butter. Repeat steps 5 more times. Top with remaining 9 half sheets of phyllo brushing each with butter. Cut into diamond shapes or squares almost through to bottom layer. Preheat oven to 325°. Bake 60 minutes. Cut completely through. Cool. Pour warm Syrup over cooled pastry. Cool.

Syrup

2 cups granulated sugar
1 cup water
¼ cup honey
2 tablespoons lemon juice
1 2-inch stick cinnamon

Bring all ingredients to boil in saucepan; reduce heat and cook 15 minutes, uncovered. Remove cinnamon stick. Stir and cool slightly.

* * *

Cookies that are to be dipped in confectioners' sugar look better if dipped twice—once while warm, again when cool.

Small Sweets

Croquembouche

Makes 6 to 7 dozen.
Preparation Time: 2 hours.

> 1 cup water
> ½ cup butter *or* margarine
> 1 cup flour
> 4 eggs
> Cream Filling
> Caramel
> Candied cherries, optional

Preheat oven to 425°. Bring water and butter to boil in heavy saucepan; add flour all at once. Stir over low heat until mixture forms ball; remove from heat. Beat in eggs, 1 at a time, beating thoroughly after each addition until smooth. Fill pastry bag, fitted with plain tip, with dough; pipe mounds, 1 inch in diameter and ½ inch high, 2 inches apart on greased baking sheets. Bake 20 minutes or until golden. Remove from pan, pierce bottom of each puff with tip of knife and cool on rack. Prepare Cream Filling; fill pastry bag fitted with star tip. Fill puffs; return to rack. Butter serving plate and metal croquembouche cone in center of plate. Dip bottom of each puff into Caramel; place around cone in layers to form pyramid. Decorate with candied cherries, if desired. Drizzle any remaining Caramel over top. Refrigerate until serving time. To serve, loosen puffs, 1 at a time, with tongs or 2 forks, starting at top.

Cream Filling

> 5 egg yolks
> ½ cup granulated sugar
> ¼ cup flour
> 2 cups milk *or* cream, heated
> 1 tablespoon Grand Marnier, Triple Sec *or* Cointreau
> 1 teaspoon vanilla

Beat egg yolks and sugar in heavy saucepan over low heat until thick and lemon colored, about 5 minutes. Add flour; stir 3 minutes. Add hot milk; increase heat and stir just to boiling or until mixture is puddinglike. Stir in liqueur and vanilla. Pour into bowl, cover with plastic wrap and chill.

Caramel

> 1½ cups granulated sugar
> ¾ cup water
> ¼ teaspoon cream of tartar

Heat all ingredients in saucepan over medium heat without stirring until mixture reaches boiling point. Lower heat; cook until clear and golden, tipping pan occasionally. Remove from heat; place saucepan in larger pan of hot water to keep syrup liquid.

Rugalah

Makes 112.
Preparation Time: 3 hours.

> 1 cup butter, softened
> 1 8-ounce package cream cheese, softened
> 2 cups flour
> Filling
> Confectioners' sugar

Preheat oven to 350°. Cream butter and cream cheese in bowl; blend in flour to make dough. Divide into 14 balls. Chill. Roll out each ball into 6-inch circle on floured board. Prepare Filling; sprinkle about 2 tablespoonfuls over dough. Pat in lightly with hands. Cut into 8 pie-shaped wedges. Starting at wide edge, roll each wedge toward point. Shape into crescent; place, pointed-seam-side down, on baking sheet. Bake 10 to 12 minutes. Cool. Sprinkle with confectioners' sugar. Store in airtight container.

Filling

> 1½ teaspoons ground cinnamon
> ½ cup granulated sugar
> ½ cup chopped nuts
> ½ cup currants

Mix all ingredients in bowl.

Cherry Cream Cheese Pastries

Makes 40.
Preparation Time: 1 hour, 15 minutes plus 4 hours to chill.

> 1 3-ounce package cream cheese, softened
> ½ cup butter *or* margarine, softened
> 1 cup flour
> ½ cup cherry preserves
> ½ cup chopped walnuts
> 1 teaspoon grated lemon rind
> Confectioners' sugar

Blend cream cheese and butter in bowl; cut into flour. Shape dough into ball. Wrap in plastic wrap; chill 3 to 4 hours. Mix preserves, nuts and rind in bowl. Divide dough in half. Roll each half ⅛ inch thick to 10 x 12-inch rectangle on lightly floured board. Cut each into 20 2½-inch squares; place ½ teaspoon preserves mixture in center of each. Moisten edges of squares with water, fold to form triangles and seal edges with fork. Place on baking sheet. Preheat oven to 375°. Bake 12 minutes. Cool on rack. Dust with confectioners' sugar. Store in airtight container in refrigerator.

Lace Wafers

Makes approximately 36.
Preparation Time: 30 minutes.

- ½ cup flour
- ½ cup finely chopped nuts
- 2 tablespoons butter
- 2 tablespoons vegetable shortening
- ¼ cup light corn syrup
- ⅓ cup light brown sugar, packed
- ¼ teaspoon vanilla or almond extract

Preheat oven to 325°. Mix flour and nuts in bowl. Melt butter and shortening in saucepan; add syrup and sugar. Bring just to a boil; remove from heat. Stir in flour-nut mixture; add vanilla. Drop by teaspoonfuls 3 inches apart on greased baking sheet. Bake 8 minutes. Cool 1 minute; remove with spatula to paper-covered rack. (If cookies are hard to remove, return to oven for a few seconds to soften.)

Meringue Mushrooms

Makes approximately 50.
Preparation Time: 2 hours plus 30 minutes chilling time.

- ½ cup confectioners' sugar
- 1 tablespoon cornstarch
- ½ cup egg whites, room temperature
- ¼ teaspoon cream of tartar
- ½ cup granulated sugar
- ½ teaspoon almond extract
- 1½ teaspoons unsweetened cocoa
- 3 ounces semisweet chocolate
- 1 tablespoon butter

Preheat oven to 200°. Mix confectioners' sugar and cornstarch in bowl. Beat egg whites in clean warm bowl until foamy; add cream of tartar and beat until soft peaks form. Gradually beat in confectioners' sugar mixture, granulated sugar and almond extract; beat until stiff, glossy peaks form. Spoon meringue into pastry bag fitted with ½-inch plain tip. Pipe 1 x ⅜-inch stems ½ inch apart on brown paper-lined baking sheet. Pipe equal number of 1½-inch round caps on another brown paper-lined baking sheet. Flatten caps slightly with moistened finger; sift cocoa over caps. Bake 1¼ hours. Turn off oven; leave baking sheets in oven to cool completely. Remove meringues from paper. Make small hollow in underside of each cap with tip of knife. Melt chocolate and butter together; place dab chocolate in hollow of cap and attach stem. Place on baking sheet. Chill 30 minutes or until chocolate is set. Pack in airtight container. Mushrooms will keep 2 to 3 days.

Date Balls

Makes approximately 36.
Preparation Time: 45 minutes.

- 2 eggs
- 1 cup granulated sugar
- 1 cup chopped dates
- 1 cup flaked coconut
- 1 cup chopped walnuts
- 1 teaspoon vanilla
- ¼ teaspoon almond extract
- Granulated sugar

Preheat oven to 350°. Beat eggs in bowl; gradually add 1 cup sugar; beat until fluffy. Add remaining ingredients except additional granulated sugar. Place in casserole. Bake 30 minutes. Stir well with wooden spoon; cool. Form into balls. Roll in additional granulated sugar. Store in airtight container.

Chocolate-Peanut Bonbons

Makes 48.
Preparation Time: 25 minutes plus chilling time.

- 2 cups confectioners' sugar
- 1 cup graham cracker crumbs or crisp rice cereal, crushed
- ½ cup flaked coconut
- ½ cup butter or margarine
- ½ cup creamy or chunk-style peanut butter
- 1 teaspoon vanilla
- 1 12-ounce package semisweet chocolate chips
- 3 tablespoons butter or vegetable shortening

Combine sugar, crumbs and coconut in bowl. Melt ½ cup butter and peanut butter in saucepan. Add vanilla; pour over dry mixture and stir to blend. Shape into 1-inch balls. Melt chocolate and butter in saucepan; coat balls with mixture. Place on waxed paper-lined tray; chill to set. Store in covered container.

* * *

To cut sticky foods, such as raisins, dates and marshmallows, use kitchen scissors dipped occasionally in hot water.

Strudel

Makes 48 slices.
Preparation Time: 2 hours, 30 minutes plus 3 hours to chill.

- 1 cup butter *or* margarine, softened
- 2 cups flour
- ¼ teaspoon salt
- 1 cup dairy sour cream
- ¼ cup graham cracker crumbs *or* fine dry bread crumbs
- 1⅓ cups pineapple, orange *or* apricot marmalade *or* combination of all three
- 1 cup flaked coconut
- 1 cup snipped golden raisins
- 1 cup chopped nuts
- ½ cup slivered maraschino cherries
- Confectioners' sugar

Cream butter in bowl; mix in flour and salt. Add sour cream; mix to form dough. Divide into 4 equal portions. Wrap each in waxed paper; chill 3 hours. Roll, 1 portion at a time, into 15 x 12-inch rectangles on lightly floured waxed paper or board. Sprinkle 1 tablespoon crumbs on each rectangle; spread with ⅓ cup marmalade, ¼ cup each coconut, raisins and nuts, and ⅛ cup cherries. Roll each rectangle jelly-roll fashion enclosing filling; pinch ends to seal. Place rolls on greased baking sheets. Slash top of each roll diagonally into 12 slices. Preheat oven to 350°. Bake 35 minutes or until golden. Place on waxed paper; slice immediately. Cool; dust with confectioners' sugar. Store loosely covered with waxed paper or foil.

Easy Apple Strudel

Makes 48 slices.
Preparation Time: 2 hours, 30 minutes plus 3 hours to chill.

- Strudel dough (see above recipe)
- 4 large tart cooking apples, peeled, cored and cut in ⅛-inch slices
- ½ cup granulated sugar mixed with 1 teaspoon ground cinnamon
- 1 teaspoon grated lemon rind
- ½ cup chopped walnuts
- ½ cup golden raisins
- ½ cup graham cracker crumbs
- Confectioners' sugar
- Whipped cream, optional

Prepare dough as directed in Strudel recipe above. Roll each portion of dough as directed. Combine remaining ingredients except confectioners' sugar and whipped cream. Spread center ⅓ of dough rectangle with ¼ filling mixture. Roll up jelly-roll fashion, starting from long end; seal edges. Repeat with remaining rectangles. Place rolls on greased baking sheet; slash at 1½-inch intervals. Preheat oven to 350°. Bake 35 minutes or until golden. Remove to rack, slice through each slash immediately and cool. Store loosely covered with waxed paper or foil. To serve, sprinkle with confectioners' sugar and top with dollop of whipped cream, if desired.

Fruit Strudel

Makes 60 slices.
Preparation Time: 2 hours.

- 8 sheets phyllo dough, thawed in wrappings
- 1 cup butter, melted
- 1 cup dry bread crumbs
- 8 cups peeled, thin apple slices *or* pitted, tart cherries
- ½ cup golden raisins
- 1 cup granulated sugar
- 1 teaspoon ground cinnamon
- Confectioners' sugar, to garnish

Preheat oven to 325°. Remove 2 phyllo sheets from package, covering remaining sheets tightly. Place 2 phyllo sheets, one on top of other, on damp tea towel. Brush with butter; sprinkle with ¼ cup crumbs. Place 2 cups apple slices or cherries and 2 tablespoons raisins on crumbs. Mix sugar and cinnamon; sprinkle ¼ on apples. Roll up from long end, pulling towel toward you and up off counter to aid in rolling pastry. Slide roll onto greased 10 x 15-inch jelly-roll pan. Cover with damp towel while finishing remaining rolls. Remove damp towel. Brush top of each strudel with melted butter. Bake 20 minutes until golden brown. Slice each roll into 15 pieces. Sprinkle with confectioners' sugar. Store loosely covered with waxed paper or foil.

Index

A
B
C
D
E
F
G
H
I
J
K
L
0
1
2
3
4
5
6
7
8
9
0
1